THE MOST BEAUTIFUL CHINESE MINDS SERIES
"最美中国人"丛书

BORN IN THE 90S: NEVER REGRETTING OUR YOUTH

出彩90后：我的青春不后悔

"最美中国人"丛书编委会 编著

U0718865

Sinolingua
华语教学出版社

First Edition 2022
Second Printing 2023

ISBN 978-7-5138-2192-6
Copyright 2022 by Sinolingua Co., Ltd
Published by Sinolingua Co., Ltd
24 Baiwanzhuang Street, Beijing 100037, China
Tel: (86)10-68320585, 68997826
Fax: (86)10-68997826, 68326333
http://www.sinolingua.com.cn
E-mail: hyjx@sinolingua.com.cn
Facebook: www.facebook.com/sinolingua
Printed by Beijing Hucais Culture Communication Co., Ltd.

Printed in the People's Republic of China

"最美中国人"丛书编委会

主　编

王君校　韩　晖

张　坤　毛　浩　董　时

编　委

韩　颖　付　眉　刘小琳　张　超

黄　勇　许　革　吴晓东　付豪杰　王荣华

编　务

马博韬

Editorial Board

Chief Editors

Wang Junxiao   Han Hui

Zhang Kun   Mao Hao   Dong Shi

Editors

Han Ying   Fu Mei   Liu Xiaolin   Zhang Chao

Huang Yong   Xu Ge   Wu Xiaodong   Fu Haojie   Wang Ronghua

Assistant Editor

Ma Botao

前言

"最美中国人"丛书以中英对照的形式向外国读者讲述新时代中国人民的奋斗故事。本丛书用细致生动的笔触介绍了志愿者、创业者、90后、普通百姓和老年人这几个不同人群中的典型故事,反映出中国人民在中国共产党的领导下实现全面小康的逐梦历程。丛书一共五册,分别是《志愿者:让爱传递到每个角落》《创业者:幸福是奋斗出来的》《出彩90后:我的青春不后悔》《平凡老百姓:把日子过出精气神儿》《中国"传家宝":那些可爱的老人们》,每册包含八到十个真实故事。为了让外国读者更加直观地了解中国社会的发展和人民生活的巨大变迁,丛书除了文字故事之外,部分故事还配有视频二维码,读者扫描二维码即可观看与文章配套的人物故事视频。

FOREWORD

"The Most Beautiful Chinese Minds" is a book series for international readers featuring stories of Chinese people from all walks of life in today's China. Presented in both Chinese and English, the series reveals the vivid and personal stories of the everyday lives of volunteers, entrepreneurs, post-90s youth, ordinary people and senior citizens as they strive to realize their own dreams and the national dream of building a moderately prosperous society in all aspects under the leadership of the Chinese Communist Party. The series includes five volumes: *Volunteers: Making the World a Better Place*, *Entrepreneurs: Striving for Happiness*, *Born in the 90s: Never Regretting Our Youth*, *Ordinary People: Living a Vibrant Life*, and *Charming Seniors: Keeping Up with the Times*. Each volume consists of eight to ten true stories about real people. It is a must-read for those wishing to better understand the true experiences of everyday Chinese people in today's China and the remarkable changes taking place in their lives. We have also provided QR codes for some stories which can link to online videos about the people from the passages.

目录 | CONTENTS

出路 ·· 1
The Way Out ·· 10

让"老手艺"焕发新生 ··· 19
Reviving *Juci* ·· 28

90后博士生的"汽车科研梦" ··· 37
A PhD Candidate's Dream of Driverless Cars ·················· 46

在无声的世界里舞蹈 ··· 53
Dancing in a Silent World ·· 63

用诗歌让乡村孩子感受爱与美 ······································· 71
Poetry Helps Rural Children Enjoy Love and Beauty ········ 82

"北斗"背后的90后 ··· 93
The Post-90s Generation Behind BDS ··························· 103

让"红旗"更加招展 ………………………… 111
Making the Hongqi (Red Flag) Car More Captivating ……… 120

好男来当兵 …………………………………… 127
A Good Man Should Join the Army ……………… 145

95后水手的海上成长日志 …………………… 161
The Deck Log of a Young Sailor ………………… 172

为家乡设计"金山银山"的姑娘 ……………… 181
A Designer Bringing Wealth to Her Hometown ……… 189

出 路

The Way Out

作者：李 玥
翻译：范逊敏

出 路

王子安永远忘不了多年前的那个下午，盲人学校的老师用很平静的语调向这群有视力障碍的少年宣告："好好学习盲人按摩，这是你们今后唯一的出路。"

"怎么可能？！"这个双目失明的男孩觉得自己突然"被推进无底的深渊"。在盲人学校的楼道里来回走了许多圈后，10岁的他决定和命运打个赌，用音乐为自己找条出路。

8年后，凭着出色的中提琴演奏，王子安收到了英国皇家伯明翰音乐学院的录取通知。2018年9月，他来到这所世界知名的音乐学府继续深造。

再把时间拉回到王子安10岁的那一天。从盲人学校回家后，他惊诧又愤怒地向父亲描述在学校的经历。"你的双手拥有选择的权利，没有什么是你做不到的。"父亲表情严肃，提高了声调。

The Way Out
出路

王子安 4 岁时，父亲就说过同样的话。那时，只有微弱光感的王子安拥有一辆四轮自行车。父亲握住他的手，带他认识自行车的龙头、座椅、踏板。王子安最喜欢从陡坡上飞驰而下，他甚至尝试过骑两轮车，但有一次栽进了半米深的池塘。

从 5 岁开始，用双手弹奏钢琴是他最幸福的事。88 个黑白键刻进了脑子里，他随时想象着自己在弹琴。遇到难啃的曲子，老师抓住他的小手在琴键上反复敲击，指尖磨破了皮，往外渗血，他痛得想哭。

"看不见怎么了？我的人生一样充满可能。"王子安用手摩擦着黑白琴键，使出全部力气按下一组和弦。

他有一双白净、瘦长的手，握起来很有力量。他从不抗拒学习按摩，他只是讨厌耳边不断重复的声音：按摩是盲人唯一的出路。

在父母为他营造的氛围里，王子安觉得自己是个再正常不过的小孩。他和别的小朋友打架，也和他们一样坐地铁、看电影、逛公园。即使被别人骂"瞎子"、被推倒在地，他也只是拍拍身上的土，心里想：瞎子可是很厉害的。

2012年，王子安尝试参加音乐院校的考试，结果他榜上无名。不过，他的考场表现吸引了中提琴主考官侯东蕾老师的注意。

"音乐对你来说意味着什么？"面试时，侯东蕾问王子安。

"生命！"这个考生高高扬起头，不假思索，给出了最"与众不同"的回答。

半年后，侯东蕾辗转联系到王子安的父亲，说自己一直在寻找这个有灵气的孩子，希望做他的音乐老师。

这位老师忘不了王子安双手落在黑白琴键上、闭着眼睛让音符流淌的场景，这本就是爱乐之人该有的模样。

听从侯东蕾老师的建议，王子安改学中提琴。弦乐难在音准，盲人敏锐的听觉反而是优势。

老师告诉他的弟子，音乐面前，人人平等，只需要用你的手去表达你的心。

但这个13岁才第一次拿起中提琴的孩子，仅仅站着都会前后摇晃，无法保持身体平衡，"当闭上眼睛，空间感消失，身体的平衡感会减弱"。为了苦练架琴的姿势，王子安常常左手举着琴，抵在肩膀上好几个小时，"骨头都要压断了"。

最开始，他连弓都拉不直。侯东蕾就花费两倍三倍的时间，握住他的手，带他一遍遍游走在琴弦上。

许多节课，老师大汗淋漓，王子安抹着眼泪。侯东蕾撂下一句"吃不了这份苦，就别走这条路"。

母亲把棉签一根根竖起粘在弦上，排成一条宽约3公分的通道。一旦碰到通道两边的棉签，王子安就知道自己没有拉成一条直线。3个月后，他终于把弓拉直了。而视力正常的学生通常1个月就能做到。

但他进步"神速"，6个月时间就从中提琴的一级跳到了九级。

学习中提琴之后，他换过4把琴，拉断过几十根弦。他调动强大的记忆力背谱子，一首长约十几分钟的曲子，通常两三天就能全部拿下。每次上课他都全程录音，不管吃饭还是睡前，他总是一遍一遍地听。好几次他拉着琴睡着了，差点儿摔倒。

奋斗的激情来自王子安的阳光心态。这个眼前总是一片漆黑的年轻人从不强调"我看不见"。他自如地使用"看"这个字，"用手摸，用鼻子闻，用耳朵听，都是我'看'的方式"。

他也不信别人说的"你只能看到黑色"，他对色彩有自己的理解：红色是刺眼的光；蓝色是大海，是水穿过手指的冰凉；绿色是树叶，密密的，像甘蔗汁的清甜味。

他学会了坐公交车从盲人学校回家，通过沿途的味道判断车开到了哪里：飘着香料味的是米粉店，混着大葱和肉香的是包子铺，水果市场依照时令充满不同的果香。

在车上，他循着声音就能找到空座位。他熟悉车子的每一个转弯，不用听报站就能准确判断下车时间。

"人尽其才，有那么难吗？"在"看"电影《无问西东》时，他安慰自己"只问努力，无问西东"，同时忍不住想象遇见梅贻琦校长，并被他录取。

当第三次报考音乐院校失败后，母亲发

现，平日里看上去没心没肺的儿子会找个角落悄悄地哭。

有人劝这家人放弃："与其把学琴的钱打了水漂儿，还不如留着给王子安养老。"

也有人建议王子安"乖乖学习盲人按摩"，毕竟盲人学校的就业率100%。

在共青团主办的广州市第二少年宫，王子安得到了很多安慰。报考音乐院校失败时，这里的同学会握住他的手，拍拍他的肩，甚至什么话也不说，只是静静陪他练琴。

广州市第二少年宫有一个由普通孩子和特殊孩子组成的融合艺术团，97人中，70%是特殊孩子。2014年，团长关小蕾在这片孕育改革气魄的土壤上先行先试，尝试融合教育。这是一种在发达国家较为成熟的教育理念，让智力障碍、视力障碍、肢体障碍等有特殊需要的孩子与普通孩子在同一课堂学习，强调每个人都有优势和弱点。

王子安成为融合艺术团的一员。在这个不以身体障碍区分"普通"和"特殊"的团队中，王子安被大家称作"中提琴王子"。

他总是耐心解答小伙伴的各种疑问,从不介意自闭症同伴讲话颠三倒四。一次,一个年龄小的孩子摔倒了,趴在地上哭,他就循着声音过去,蹲下来鼓励他自己站起来。同样,当王子安需要去洗手间时,总会有人牵起他的手,给他指引。

"就像真正的朋友那样,"他的表情严肃起来,"寻求相似,接纳不同。"

在关小蕾看来,只需要创造一个融合的环境,孩子们就会在相处中发现:身体障碍者需要支持,就像近视的人需要眼镜一样简单。这也是王子安一直以来所认同的理念。

在融合艺术团,王子安和他的伙伴们挽着手登上过广州著名的星海音乐厅,也曾受邀去美国、加拿大、瑞士、法国等国家演出。他们中有人声音高、有人声音低,但不妨碍每个人同等地享受音乐的快乐。

"虽然我看不见这个世界,但我要让世界看见我的奋斗。"在一次去异国演出的途中,他吹着太平洋的风,挥动帽子高声喊。

这是让关小蕾流泪的一个画面。她常告诉艺术团的孩子,其实人人都有障碍,只是有轻有重，有人可以掩藏，有人显露在外。

"我们创造融合环境，是为了让每个孩子都相信努力奋斗的意义，都能毫无惧色地拥抱未来。"

经历种种内心的磨砺，王子安在18岁这年，依旧将音乐这条出路作为自己的成人礼。

2017年11月，王子安站在了英国皇家伯明翰音乐学院考官面前。他穿着母亲为他准备的黑色衬衫和裤子，还特意用啫喱抓了抓头发。花了半个小时，他拉完了准备好的4首曲子。

"虽然这不是最后的决定，"面试官迫不及待地把评语读给他听，"因为你出众的表现，我会为你争取最高的奖学金。"

"我赢了！"灿烂的阳光下，他在心里放声大笑。

The Way Out

Wang Zi'an still remembered that afternoon many years ago, the teacher of the school for the blind claimed to the group of visually impaired teenagers in a very calm tone, "It's best if you learn massage. This is the only way out for you."

"I can't believe that!" The blind boy felt he had suddenly been "pushed into a bottomless pit". After pacing through the hallways of the school several times, the 10-year-old boy decided to make a bet with fate and use music as his "way out."

Eight years later, after an excellent viola performance, Wang Zi'an received an acceptance letter to be enrolled at the Royal Birmingham Conservatoire in the UK. In September 2018 he came to this world-renowned conservatoire to continue his studies.

Back when Wang Zi'an was 10 years old, he returned home from the school for the blind and indignantly told his father what the teacher had said. His father looked at him and said in a serious tone, "What you do with your hands is your choice. There is nothing you cannot do."

His father had said the same thing when Wang Zi'an was four. At that time, young Wang could only faintly sense light. He owned a bicycle with two training wheels. His father took his hand to touch the bicycle to help him know about the handlebar, the seat and the pedals, and he encouraged him to ride it. Wang loved to ride the bike, and especially loved speeding down slopes. He even tried riding it without the training wheels, but he fell into a shallow pond once.

At the age of five, he began to play the piano. He regarded it as the happiest thing. The eighty-eight black and white keys were carved into his mind, and he imagined himself playing the piano all the time. When encountering a difficult piece, the teacher would grab his little hand and push the correct keys again and again. He would practice so much that his fingertips would bleed. It was so painful that he wanted to cry.

"Though I can't see, my life has so many possibilities," he thought to himself at the time. When touching the piano keys, he played chords with all his emotion.

He had white, thin hands, but they were strong. He did not resist the idea of learning massage, but he hated hearing that it was the only way out for him.

His parents treated him as a perfectly normal child. As a boy, he fought with other kids, took the subway, went to the movies and to the park. He could do anything other boys could do. Even if someone teased him by calling him "blind boy" or pushed him to the ground, he'd just stand up, pat the dust off his clothes, and go on about his way, thinking being blind did not make me anything less.

In 2012, he tried to take the exam for a conservatoire, but he failed. But his performance attracted the attention of viola teacher Hou Donglei.

"What does music mean to you?" Hou asked the boy.

Without even thinking, Wang held his head up high and replied, "Life!"

Half a year later, Hou contacted Wang's father, and said he had been looking for the inspired child, hoping to be his music teacher.

What impressed the teacher most was how Wang closed his eyes and enjoyed the music as he played. The teacher believed this was the appearance of someone who truly loved music.

Following Hou Donglei's advice, Wang switched to the viola. He said it was very difficult to properly tune the viola, but blind people tended to possess more acute hearing than normal people.

The teacher told his students that everyone was equal before music; the only thing you needed to do was to use your hands to play what your heart felt.

But when the 13-year-old boy first picked up the viola, he was unable to keep balance, weaving back and forth as he stood. "When you close your eyes, the sense of space disappears, and your sense of balance weakens," Wang said. In order to practice the posture, he would hold the viola on his shoulder for hours. "It felt like my bones were being broken."

At first, he couldn't even keep the bow straight. Hou spent many lessons with him, teaching him by holding his hand and leading him again and again.

During many classes, Hou would sweat profusely, trying to teach as

Wang would break down in tears. One day, Hou said, "If you can't bear the pain, then you can't take this road."

Wang's mother had an idea. She stuck cotton swabs on the strings one by one and arranged them into spaces about 3 centimeters wide. As soon as Wang touched a swab, he knew he was not bowing in a straight line. After three months, he finally could bow straight. For students with normal vision, this usually took about a month.

After overcoming this obstacle, Wang made rapid progress, jumping from Level One to Level Nine within six months.

During this time, he changed four violas and broke dozens of strings. He used his good memory to memorize the compositions. For example, it would take him two or three days to memorize a ten-minute-long piece. He would record every class and listen to it over and over again at dinner or before going to bed. Sometimes he'd fall asleep while playing the viola and would nearly fall over.

The passion for practice comes from his positive attitude. This young man, who is always in complete darkness, never focuses on being unable to see. He uses the word "see" quite often, but it has a different meaning for him. "Touching with my hands, smelling with my nose, hearing with my ears… that is the way I see."

He also does not agree when people say to him, "You can only see black." He has his own concept of color; red is dazzling light; blue is the sea, and cold water running through your fingers; green is the leaves, and it is dense like the sweetness of sugarcane juice.

He also learned how to take the bus home from school. He would know his location according to the smells along the way: the spicy rice noodle shop, the steamed stuffed bun shop with its mix of scallions and meat, the fruit market with its seasonal variety of aromas.

On the bus, he could find an empty seat by listening to the sound of emptiness. Once seated, he knew every turn of the bus as it followed its route, and could tell exactly when to get off without listening to the stop announcement.

"Is it so hard to make the best use of one's talents?" he thought. When "watching" the movie *Forever Young*, he comforted himself that "I only care about hard work and stay young at heart, and I don't care about other things." He couldn't help imagining himself as a person in the movie meeting and being admitted by President Mei Yiqi of Tsinghua University.

When he applied for the third time to the conservatoire and failed, his mother found him crying in the corner.

Some people told Wang's parents to persuade him to give up. "It's better to save the money for the rest of his life than to spend it in playing the viola."

Someone also suggested that Wang should focus on learning massage, saying that at least with this skill he could find a job.

Wang went to study music at the Second Children's Palace in Guangzhou, an institution where children could take part in various extracurricular activities. When he failed admission to the music school for the third time, the students there were very kind to him, holding his hand, patting his shoulder, and saying nothing as they quietly accompanied him to practice the viola.

There is an art troupe composed of ordinary and disabled children in the Second Children's Palace in Guangzhou. Of the 97 children, 70 percent are disabled. In 2014, Guan Xiaolei, the leader of the art troupe, tried to integrate some new reforms in the field of education, reforms which were a relatively mature educational concept in developed countries. Children with special needs, such as intellectual, visual and physical disabilities, were taught in the same classroom with ordinary children, showing that everyone had strengths and weaknesses, and that everyone was equal.

Wang became a member of the art troupe, in which there was no difference between "ordinary" and "special" children based on physical disabilities, Wang was known as the "Prince of the Viola". He was always patient to answer questions raised by other students, including autistic children who had trouble speaking. Once, when a younger child fell to the ground and was crying, Wang followed the sound and squatted down next to him to encourage him to get up. Similarly, when Wang needed to go to the bathroom, someone would always hold his hand and show him the way.

"Just like true friends," Wang said, "we sought similarities and accepted our differences."

In Guan Xiaolei's view, inclusive environments like this facilitate understanding and empathy. Children will find that the disabled need support, just as short-sighted people need glasses. Wang also agrees with this philosophy.

In the Art Troupe, Wang and his friends performed in the famous Xinghai Concert Hall in Guangzhou, and have also performed in other countries such as the United States, Canada, Switzerland, and France. Everyone in the troupe has their own characteristics, but that does not prevent anyone from enjoying the music.

"Although I cannot see the world, I want the world to see my hard work," Wang said. On the way to a performance in a foreign country, he waved and shouted loudly as the Pacific wind blew on his face.

It was a scene that moved Ms. Guan Xiaolei to tears. She'd often tell the children in the art troupe that everyone has his own troubles; some are slight and some are serious. Some people can hide them while others can't. "We create an inclusive environment so that every child can perceive and believe in the value of hard work and face the future without fear."

At the age of 18, after many tribulations, Wang still regarded music as his life's pursuit.

In November 2017 Wang stood in front of examiners at the Royal Birmingham Conservatoire, wearing a black shirt and trousers that his mother had bought for him. For the next thirty minutes, he performed the four pieces.

After listening, an examiner said to him, "This is not the final decision, but because of your outstanding performance, I will seek the maximum scholarship for you."

He was overjoyed. "I made it!" he thought to himself as he left the building and walked out into the bright sunshine.

The Way Out
出路

Scan for a Video

让"老手艺"焕发新生

Reviving *Juci*

作者：朱娟娟
翻译：李冰青

让"老手艺"焕发新生

"啪嗒"一声脆响,随着手中最后一颗锔钉完好地嵌入锔钉孔内,赵凤林满意地笑了。他手上的那把茶壶上,46颗锔钉匀称地在壶身上勾勒出一弯弦月。

打碎的瓷器被用像订书钉一样的金属"锔子"重新修复起来——锔瓷,是中国最古老的瓷器修复技艺。这项技艺始于宋代,《清明上河图》上就有手艺人锔瓷的情景。

踏入锔瓷这个行当第6年,传统技艺在这位90后手里重新鲜活起来。从蜗居在五六平方米的宿舍一遍遍练习技艺,到如今开办自己的工作室,赵凤林的业务延伸至20多个省市,"锔瓷成就了艺术品,也帮我成就了自己"。

埋头习艺

赵凤林出生在广西一个工匠世家。他

从小见识过不少老手艺，锔瓷也不例外。那时，祖辈担着工具走街串巷吆喝，有时也赶大集揽生意，"老手艺人迫于生计赶场子，更多情况考虑实用性，不太在乎美观"。

2013年，赵凤林在朋友的推荐下到武汉学习茶艺。泡茶时偶尔会有器物损坏，一些比较名贵的茶具丢掉非常可惜，赵凤林萌生了重拾祖辈锔瓷手艺的想法。

说干就干，他白天在茶楼上班，晚上回到住处钻研锔瓷技艺，一遍遍练习钻孔和上锔钉。为激励自己锔瓷的胆识，赵凤林甚至亲手把心爱的紫砂杯摔碎，再用4天时间一钉一钉地锔好。2014年，赵凤林辞职，全身心投入锔瓷技艺的钻研中。

"差不多一年没有任何收入。"赵凤林当时租住在一个五六平方米的厨房里，只够放下一张工作台，他托人打出半个吊顶当床。

生活条件艰苦在醉心锔瓷的赵凤林看来不算什么，但练习材料的匮乏着实让他痛苦万分。赵凤林不得不去跟人家求各种废弃的残破器件，修好了还回去还要感谢人家的信任。他经常连续一两个月埋头练习一种工艺，逐渐熟悉了找碴、对缝、锔钉、钻孔等工序，并找到了属于自己的感觉。

"每个师傅的感觉不一样，都会找到自己合适控制的钻孔角度和力度。"赵凤林坦言，手艺和工业化生产的不同之处就在于独一无二，一个师傅修不出一模一样的两件作品，锔钉有瘦长的，有饱满的，一切随器物的自然形态而定。

在赵凤林的收藏柜上，他的处女作放在一个并不太显眼的位置，但在他心中，这件台湾陶水壶的分量非同寻常。整件水壶锔钉160颗，打孔320个，密集处每颗钉间距不到两毫米，赵凤林做了整整半个月才完成，那时他才学了8个多月。"这个壶的锔钉大小差别很大，因为它是一个煮水壶，锔钉抓力不够会漏水，要用大钉；又因为它的壶嘴、壶盖有缺失，又必须用小钉。反复量了几次，才把各处钉的大小确定妥当。"

功夫不负有心人，赵凤林的锔瓷技艺

越来越精湛。从口径30厘米的花瓶到不足5厘米的小茶杯，从瓷器、紫砂到玉器、琉璃，赵凤林用金、银、铜、铁、锡，珠、玉、石等材料，运用手艺与创造力，对器物的缺损部分进行"锔补"。

赵凤林在锔瓷领域的钻研和探索被人看在眼里。2014年，在政府部门的帮助下，赵凤林在武汉汉阳造创意产业园第一次有了一个正式工位，免除一年租金。随着他的手艺在圈子里口口相传，他的生意越来越好。

2017年，他将工作室开到汉口一处茶叶市场里。工作室投资10多万元，包含门面租金、工具设备、家具等。修补一件瓷器，按照锔钉材质、修复工艺不同，收费从一两百元到几千元不等。

重赋生命

在赵凤林看来，无论是价值数十万元的宋代建盏还是普通茶杯，并无高低贵贱之分，它们都饱含着情分。"许多爱瓷器的人，一件东西相伴几十年。每件器物都有自己的生命，而修复，就是重生。"

一次，一位70多岁的老先生捧着一只破损的大瓷碗来，要求不惜用银钉锔并镶上漂亮的花钉。原来，这只碗是老先生已故夫人当年的嫁妆。夫人故去，这只瓷碗承载着浓浓的情思。赵凤林非常慎重，他小心翼翼地测量瓷碗的尺寸，揣摩锔钉的位置，力求让每一颗银钉的大小、宽窄、间距都与整个瓷碗的气韵相适宜。考虑到它是结婚嫁妆，赵凤林用金属钻刻工艺钻了一个"喜"字，将之镶嵌在碎片缺失的位置。老先生收到后，激动地打电话向赵凤林表示感谢："多亏了你，我心里的遗憾终于补好了。"

在赵凤林看来，随着人们物质条件与审美水平的提高，锔瓷技艺不能停留在老一辈"补实了、不漏水"的阶段，要更进一步——不仅做到还原器物形态，更要加入对美的不同理解，让产品成为艺术品。现在，茶文化正慢慢渗透到年轻人的生活中，赵凤林抓住年轻人追求精致与个性的心理，设计出很多精美小巧、韵味各异的锔钉纹饰，蜻蜓、荷花、祥云……他把传统手艺的智慧和古典文化的内涵倾注在一件件残碎的器物中——一把金刚钻让它们又"活"了过来。

2018年6月，27岁的赵凤林作为武汉最年轻的锔瓷非遗传承人，被选拔参加国家艺术基金"古陶瓷修复青年人才培养项目"。他深知应肩负起弘扬锔瓷技艺的重任，让传统手艺在90后手中重焕光彩。

严谨的年轻人

"至今，我也不敢说自己出师了。"在工作室里沏上一杯茶，赵凤林缓缓地说。在他看来，慢工才能出细活儿，急不得，躁不得。而得到赵凤林认可并且坚持留下来的徒弟，只有陈然、张伟、张秋玲三个同为90后的年轻人。

他们从镶锔钉学起，这在锔瓷的各项工艺中属于最简单的一类，即便如此，也需要反反复复钻至少200个孔、锔100个钉，才能够对钉与瓷之间的微妙关系有所把握。

赵凤林经常跟徒弟们说，唯有一点一滴地积累，用心揣摩技艺，才可能有日后熟能生巧之杰作。而徒弟张秋玲则感慨，社会上有各种各样的速成班，一个星期就教会一门技术，很多年轻人只图快、不求精，"做锔瓷是不一样的，进入这行，3个月也只能说知道怎么做。跟着赵老师学一两年，才逐渐找到自己擅长的那一种手法。"大师兄陈然擅长做锔钉，他做的锔钉不仅美观耐用，而且排布匀称合理；二师兄张伟擅长铜器镂空技艺，寥寥几笔就能刻画出鹤、荷、水的神韵。

"90后有90后的想法和创新。"赵凤林说，好多年轻人想创业，有一个男孩在他这里学了一个月就回家乡开自己的工作室了。赵凤林希望有更多的年轻人来学习锔瓷手艺，但他更期望当下的年轻人能慢下来，潜心揣摩瓷的质感和钉的美感，安安静静地将手中的工作做好。

在这间名为"匠林"意在"希望能将锔瓷手艺传播开来,在脚下这片土地上蔚然成林"的工作室外,大街上汽车呼啸而过,行人脚步匆匆。而室内,年轻的师徒伏在桌前,专注着手头的活计。只听得"铛——铛——",金刚钻与锔钉碰撞发出的声响在袅袅青烟中回荡。

Reviving *Juci*

With a final "Clang!" Zhao Fenglin hammered the last metal staple into the hole and smiled with satisfaction. In his hand, 46 staples symmetrically outlined the shape of a crescent moon on the fragile broken porcelain teapot.

This method of repairing broken porcelain by "stapling" cracks and broken porcelain pieces together with casted metal staples is called "*juci*," and it is the oldest ceramic/porcelain repair technique in China. It originated during the Song Dynasty (960-1279), and it is actually depicted in the famous Song Dynasty painting *Along the River During the Qingming Festival* where *juci* craftsmen can be seen repairing porcelain.

Juci craftsmen usually follows five steps: (1) Craftsman matches the broken pieces together to see how the porcelain is supposed to look like in its intact condition; (2) Decide the number and the location of possible nailing staples; (3) Use a diamond bit to drill holes on the surface; (4) Cast suitable metal staples; (5) Apply clay powder and egg-white on the surface to assure no visible cracks exist.

During his sixth year of being a *juci* craftsman, these ancient traditional skills have been brought back to life in the hands of this young man born in the nineties. From his practicing *juci* over and over again in his tiny dorm room to now having his own studio, Zhao's business currently extends to more than 20 provinces and cities. But as Zhao said, "*juci* reconstructs the porcelain, but it has also helped reconstruct me."

Learning *Juci*

Zhao was born into a family of artisans in Guangxi Zhuang Autonomous Region. He grew up seeing *juci* as well as many other old craft techniques. At that time, craftsmen would walk through streets and alleyways with their tools and yell out their profession, hoping to solicit business. "The old craftsmen needed to earn a living, so in most cases they were more concerned with functionality than aesthetics when repairing broken porcelain."

In 2013, a friend recommended Zhao go to Wuhan to study the art of the Chinese tea ceremony. Zhao noticed that expensive tea sets would sometimes be damaged while making tea. He thought it was a pity to throw the sets away, and this gave him the idea to study *juci* from his elderly relatives.

Zhao worked in the teahouse by day, and studied *juci* at night, repeatedly practicing drilling and hammering the metal staples. To motivate himself, he even broke his favorite zisha cup and repaired it by hand, staple by staple, which took him four days. In 2014, he quit his job and devoted himself to becoming a *juci* craftsman.

"I didn't have any income for almost a year." He could only afford to rent a small room about the size of a kitchen, which only had a workbench. He hired someone to build a bed suspended from the ceiling where he could sleep.

The difficult living conditions did not bother him; his biggest obstacle was his lack of work materials. He would go around and often ask people for unwanted ceramics in order to practice his craft, and return the repaired porcelain to the owners without asking for money. He would bury himself in work for months, learning how to find cracks and put broken pieces together, drill holes, make metal staples. Over time he gradually developed his repair style.

"Every craftsman works in different ways, and everybody will find their own drilling angle and force with which they are comfortable," he said. "Uniqueness makes handicrafts different from industrial production. Even the same craftsman cannot make two identical pieces. Metal staples can be long or short, and each of them is cast according to the original shape of the porcelain."

Inside his cabinet was his very first work, a piece of Taiwan pottery. It was placed inconspicuously, but this piece was special for Zhao. He'd only been learning *juci* for about eight months when he repaired it, and it took him two weeks to complete. He drilled 320 holes and used about 160 metal staples. For severely broken areas, metal staples were lined up next to each other with gaps less than 2mm apart. "The size of metal staples used in this repair is drastically different. Large ones are used to mend the body of the pottery since they will apply more force to 'clip' the body together, stopping water leakage. However, the mouth and the lid need smaller metal staples for more refined restoration. I had to measure many times before finalizing the size of each metal staple."

His attention to detail and hard work paid off. Over time, Zhao's craftsmanship became more and more exquisite. He now could utilize gold, silver, copper, iron, tin, beads, jade, and stone to repair defective porcelain, zisha pots and jade wares, no matter the size.

Zhao's research and work in porcelain restoration was highly regarded. In 2014, with the help of government departments, he opened a studio at Hanyang Creative Industrial Park where he was exempted one year's rent. As his reputation passed through word of mouth, his business was getting better and better.

In 2017, he moved his studio to a tea market in Hankou and invested more than 100,000 yuan on studio decoration, furniture, and porcelain restoration equipment. He charged from 100 yuan to several thousand, depending on the needs of the restoration and the techniques and metal staples he must use.

Bringing the Broken Back to Life

In Zhao's opinion, whether it was a Song Dynasty piece worth hundreds of thousands of yuan or an ordinary teacup, every piece of porcelain was priceless because of the affection for it by the owner. "People who love porcelain have probably had it for decades. Every object has its own life. As a *juci* craftsman, my job is to bring these beloved objects back to life."

Once, an old gentleman in his seventies came to Zhao with a damaged porcelain bowl and requested he use silver staples to repair it. The bowl was part of the dowry of this old gentleman's late wife. After his wife had passed away, the porcelain bowl was what he had left of her memory. Hearing this story, Zhao was very careful when repairing the bowl. He carefully measured the size and chose the location for each possible drill hole to make sure the repair would perfectly match the style and the charm of the original bowl. Considering that the bowl was part of a wedding dowry, he made a silver ornament in the shape of the character *xi*, the Chinese character meaning "happiness" and often used in marriages, and inlaid it on the surface where broken porcelain pieces were missing. After receiving it, the old gentleman called Zhao to express his gratitude, saying emotionally, "The regret in my heart is finally repaired."

Zhao believes that as people's material conditions and aesthetic standards continue to improve, *juci* should not simply be for "mending and fixing," but rather shift its focus back to aesthetic creativity to revive the Chinese art of porcelain repair so that not only the shape of the porcelain is restored, but it is also "recast" as a piece of art. Currently, tea culture is gradually infiltrating the younger generation in China. More and more young people buy teapots and teacups. Zhao has grasped their pursuit for refinement and individuality, and he designs metal staples with various decorated patterns such as dragonflies, lotus flowers and auspicious clouds to make repaired teacups look special and attractive to young customers. He pours his wisdom of traditional craftsmanship and classical culture into these repaired pieces and uses diamond drilling bits to make them "live" again.

In June 2018, 27-year-old Zhao, as one of the youngest inheritors of *juci* techniques in Wuhan, was selected to participate in the Ancient Ceramic Restoration Craftsmanship Training Program sponsored by the China National Arts Fund (CNAF). He has been fully aware of his responsibility for carrying forward the *juci* techniques to help this traditional skill shine again in the hands of the 90s generation.

Rigorous Young Man

"To this day I don't dare to proclaim to be a master," he said while making himself a cup of tea in the studio. In his view, a *juci* craftsman needed to be patient; only by working slowly could one produce fine artwork. Many had come to him wanting to be his apprentice, but those approved by Zhao were only Chen Ran, Zhang Wei, and Zhang Qiuling – also all born in the 90s.

They started by learning to drill holes and inlay metal staples, which were the simplest among all the techniques needed to learn. Even so, they still needed to drill at least 200 times and inlay 100 metal staples in order to grasp the delicate relationship between the metal staples and the porcelain.

Zhao often tells his apprentices that experience comes from practice, and practice makes perfect. Zhang Qiuling, one of the three apprentices, said, "There are all kinds of short-term courses now claiming to teach you a crafting skill in one week. Many young people do this because they want to learn quickly and don't care to truly master the technique. *Juci* is different. After three months, you merely know the general procedure. I have gradually developed my own way of repair work after studying with Master Zhao for two years." Another apprentice, Chen Ran, was good at casting metal staples. The metal staples he made were functional and pleasing to the eye, and the way he aligned them was well-proportioned and reasonable. The other apprentice Zhang Wei was good at making copper ornaments depicting cranes, lotuses, and the shape of water with just a few strokes.

"People born in the 90s have many creative and innovative ideas," Zhao said. "Many young people want to start their own businesses. Once, there was a young man who only studied with me for a month and then returned home to open his own studio." Zhao hoped that more young people would be willing to learn *juci*, but he also hoped that they could learn step by step and take the time to figure out the texture of porcelain and the aesthetics of porcelain restoration.

Zhao had named his studio Jianglin — "Jiang" for craftsman and "Lin" for forest, which represented his wish to "revive old *juci* craftsmanship in China in the hopes that more people will carry it forward."

Outside his studio, cars roared by and pedestrians walked quickly. Inside the studio, the master and his apprentices sat quietly in front of the table, focusing on the work at hand. All you could hear are the "clang, clang, clang" of the diamond bit drilling into the porcelain, echoing through the curling smoke.

Reviving *Juci*

让"老手艺"焕发新生

Scan for a Video

90后博士生的"汽车科研梦"

A PhD Candidate's Dream of Driverless Cars

作者：叶雨婷
翻译：吴爱俊

90后博士生的"汽车科研梦"

2018年10月14日晚上,厦门大学的体育场内座无虚席,一场创业盛会正在这里举行。主持人大声宣布:"第四届中国大学生'互联网'创新创业大赛的全国总冠军是北京理工大学项目'中云智车——未来商用无人车行业定义者'!"此时此刻,这个项目的负责人倪俊不禁长舒了一口气。对于场下的近万名观众而言,这个年轻人谈吐成熟,带来的项目无懈可击,得到冠军并不令人意外。

和其他团队不同,倪俊的团队只有他自己一个人来厦门参加比赛。因为团队的其他成员都太忙了,不仅要忙学业,还要忙着准备2018年11月的中国大学无人驾驶方程式赛车比赛。大学生创新创业大赛结束的当天,倪俊匆匆与厦门市谈妥了项目落地及投资引进的事宜,第二天就踏上了回京路。

生于1992年的倪俊总透着和同龄人不

一样的成熟，和人交谈时没有半点儿含糊或"不得体"；他对团队成员的要求也十分严格。当然，有时候他的那些"不破不立"的做法还是能让人看到年轻人的冲劲儿的。

90后男孩的汽车梦

在厦门的几场比赛中，倪俊每次介绍自己简历的时候都会引起台下一阵阵的赞叹声。作为北京理工大学的在读博士，他已经出版了两部专著，发表了SCI/EI论文数十篇，拥有发明专利近30项，曾作为唯一的90后入选2016中国科协青年人才托举工程，并入选2016中国汽车工程学会青年人才托举工程，获2013中国青少年科技创新奖、2017北京市青年五四奖章。

一系列的光环，源于这个男孩的汽车梦。

"和很多小男孩一样，我从小就喜欢汽车。"2009年，刚参加完高考的倪俊估分填报志愿时便选择了北京理工大学的车辆工程系。神奇的是，他的实际高考成绩和自己估的分数一样，他如愿以偿地来到北京继续自己的汽车梦。

"那时候太小了，17岁，谈不上有什么'远大理想'，只是想做自己喜欢的事。"倪俊回想着当年的情景微笑着说。

当时，方程式赛车刚刚引入中国不久，跟北理工平行的很多重点工科院校都投入到了研发之中。一个很偶然的机会，倪俊接触到了学校的方程式赛车队，随即他就对方程式赛车的研究产生了浓浓的兴趣。从那时起，倪俊就利用课余时间自学了本专业本科到博士的所有课程，还阅读了大量国内外汽车动力学领域的著作及文献。

2011年，他进入了人才济济的方程式赛车工作室。于是，在这个北理工北门附近一个近1000平方米的工程训练基地，他一做就是七年。

当时，这个研究领域在国内刚刚开辟，还远没有形成完整的理论体系，一时间倪俊和队友们陷入了深深的迷茫之中。"就像是老师给你留作业，却没有告诉你公式。"为了建构一个适用于北理工方程式赛车队的理论体系，倪俊开始了为期一年半的苦读生涯：早上五六点钟起来，夜里一两点钟睡觉；不论寒暑，没有假期。

几年来，倪俊和团队的成果越来越多，这个基地也随之扩建，但他的作息一直没变。在这个像简易厂房的基地中，如今已排列了好几台无人车，有些卸下了轮子还在调试，几个无人车通用底盘则是团队如今正在创业的"明星产品"。

"无人驾驶技术对我国国民经济发展与国防安全建设有着重要的战略意义。我们能否掌握无人驾驶核心技术，关系到在这一次世界智能汽车产业变革升级的历史机遇中，我国能否实现'汽车大国'向'汽车强国'的迈进之梦，更关系到我国未来新一代陆军装备发展的强军梦想。"在此次大赛的闭幕式中，倪俊作为冠军代表参赛学生发言时这样说。

为中国汽车事业奋斗

按倪俊的话说，"年轻人嘛，会为了梦想而冲动。"看上去十分沉稳的倪俊，冲动起来也做了不少"破天荒"的事。

2012年、2016年及2017年,倪俊三次随队携中国第一辆燃油赛车、中国第一辆电动赛车、中国第一辆无人驾驶赛车赴德国参赛,分别实现了中国燃油赛车、电动赛车、无人驾驶赛车在世界最高舞台的首次亮相。2017年,倪俊率队研发世界首辆无人驾驶赛车,并配合中国汽车工程学会创办"中国大学生无人驾驶方程式汽车大赛",倪俊担任规则主要制定者及赛事运营者。

按他的话说,年轻人总会对"第一"有种执念。

"2016年,我们正在研发无人驾驶赛车,当时听说有别的国家也在做这件事,我们就想一定要争个'第一',让世界第一辆无人驾驶赛车是由我们中国人研发的。于是,没日没夜地熬了很多天,我们终于研发出世界第一辆无人驾驶赛车。"倪俊说,"其实,我们团队经常会做这样一些事,为了我们的信仰,我们不惜一切,为了我们的国家,我们更不惜一切。"

年轻,对于倪俊来说,就是有信仰与

冲劲儿，就是要在20多岁的时候做一些顶天立地的事情。两年前，倪俊要赴黑龙江漠河，他的团队研发的军用无人车"地面航母"将在那里参加"跨越险阻"军方无人车比赛。大雾弥漫，能见度只有几米，倪俊驾车在大兴安岭艰难行进，为的是将一块峰值功率300kW、40C超高放电倍率的钴酸锂电池送达现场。

"这个电池危险性高，所以我不敢把它交给任何一个运输机构转运。所以，我自己租了一辆商务车，把后座卸了，装着这300公斤的'炸弹'，从北京往返漠河7000公里，开了六天六夜完成任务。"倪俊说。

"因为怕家人担心，当时我没有告诉他们。那时候的大兴安岭里大雾弥漫，道路坑洼不平，电池如果出现危险，杀伤力很大，现在回想起来仍有些后怕。"倪俊感慨地回忆道。

为了理想不断前行

在倪俊看来，将自己的科研成果实现产

业化并真正服务于国民经济发展是十分必要和值得的。

"学术往往存在于论文上，但我想要让学术成果实现产业应用，真正为国民经济发展做出贡献。同时，我们想把北理工学生科技创新的格局再往前推进一步，从创新到创业，在国家双创的大潮下实现科技成果转化。"倪俊说。

2018年2月，团队启动了"中云智车"项目，将团队在赛车领域所积累的技术及经验应用于从事特定场景无人车的整车研发、生产和运营，目前已推出小型通用全线控底盘"中云1.0"等一系列成果，在北京国际车展、世界智能车挑战赛等展会上均有亮相，也让他们一举获得了第四届全国大学生"互联网"创新创业大赛的全国总冠军。

据了解，"中云智车"已经形成了无人车整车研发与生产的新模式，推动无人物流车、无人摆渡车、无人运货车、无人军用车等特定场景无人车的产业化应用。目前，团队已与多家物流电商、大型工业园区达成战略合作，生产基地完成建设，预计年产能超

1200台。

得奖后，倪俊如今备受媒体追捧。在倪俊看来，这份荣誉属于这七年来帮助过他们的每一位老师，属于这七年来与自己并肩奋斗过的每一名战友。他希望在博士毕业后能够继续留校从事无人车的科研工作，并和团队一起努力将"中云智车"发展成为学校的学科性产业化项目，"在未来，为我们学校无人车领域的产学研一体化发展，乃至中国的智能汽车产业发展，贡献我们毕生的力量"。

"但行好事，不问前程。"倪俊这样展望自己的未来。

A PhD Candidate's Dream of Driverless Cars

It was the evening of October 14, 2018, and the Xiamen University stadium was packed to full capacity. But an entrepreneurship competition was held here. The host announced loudly, "The champion of the 4th China College Students' Internet Innovation and Entrepreneurship Competition is the project launched by the Beijing Institute of Technology — the 'Zhongyun Smart Vehicle Project' — a pioneering project focusing on the future industry of commercial driverless cars!" At this moment, winning project coordinator Ni Jun heaved a long sigh. In the eyes of nearly ten thousand spectators present, the young, mature man had submitted an impeccable project, and all believed his team truly deserved the award.

Ni Jun was the only member of his team to attend the competition. His other team members were too busy with their study and were also preparing for the upcoming Chinese University Formula Driverless Car Race in November 2018. The day the competition ended, he quickly negotiated an agreement with the Xiamen municipal government on his winning project's implementation and investment. The next day, he returned to Beijing.

Ni Jun was born in 1992, but he looked more mature than his peers. When talking with others, he could express his views explicitly and properly. He was also strict with his team members. His boldness reflected the young man's strong desire to make a breakthrough.

A Boy's Driverless Car Dream

During the Xiamen competition, his self-introduction would illicit the admiration and applause from the audience. As a PhD candidate at the Beijing Institute of Technology, he had already published two monographs and dozens of essays in SCI/EI journals. He also owned nearly 30 patents. He was the only 90's generation young man selected into the 2016 China Association of Science and Technology Young Talents Cultivation Project and 2016 China Society of Automotive Engineers Young Talents Cultivation Project. In 2013 he was awarded the China Youth Science and Technology Innovation Award, and in 2017 he won the Beijing Youth May 4 Medal.

All his achievements could be attributed to this boy's car dream.

"Like many boys, I was very fond of cars," he said. When he took the national college entrance exam in 2009, he chose the Department of Vehicular Engineering of the Beijing Institute of Technology as his preferred school. His exam results turned out to be exactly as he'd predicted, and he was admitted to the institute to continue his pursuit of his car dream.

"At that time, I was 17 years old, and I never really considered 'big ideals'. I just wanted to do what I liked," said Ni Jun with a smile while recalling his past.

At that time, formula car racing had just been introduced into China, and the Beijing Institute of Technology was actively investing in research and development of formula cars, along with many other key engineering universities. By chance, Ni Jun came into contact with the

BIT formula car team, and immediately showed a keen interest in the research project. Once enrolled at BIT, he was very disciplined in his study during his undergraduate, postgraduate and PhD years, spending all his spare time studying and also reading a wide range of articles and books from home and abroad in the field of vehicle dynamics.

In 2011, he joined the Formula Racing Studio, a training site located near the north gate of BIT and covering nearly 1,000 square meters. His seven years' research began.

At that time, research in this field just started in China, and there was still a long way to go before a comprehensive theoretical system could be formed. For quite a while, Ni Jun and his team members were very confused, like "a teacher leaving homework for you without telling you the formula," as he put it. In order to establish a theoretical system appropriate for the BIT racing team, Ni Jun spent a year and a half studying hard. He'd get up at five or six o'clock in the morning and sleep at one or two o'clock at night. No matter how hot or cold, rain or shine, he never took a break.

In recent years, Ni Jun and his team have made great achievements, and the base has also been expanded. But his disciplined routine had never changed. Nowadays, you could see many driverless cars lined up at the site still being tested, and some chassis had great potential to be their "star products".

During his victory speech at the closing ceremony, Ni Jun said, "Self-driving technology is of strategic importance to the Chinese economy and to China's national security. The mastery of this core technology is vital for China to transform itself from simply being a large car

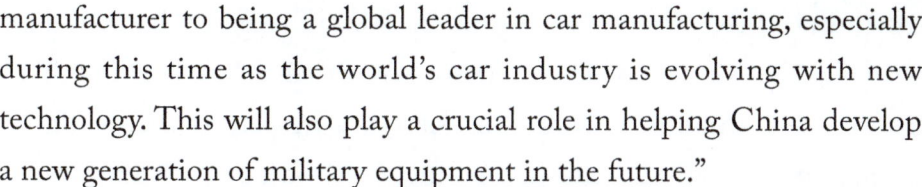

manufacturer to being a global leader in car manufacturing, especially during this time as the world's car industry is evolving with new technology. This will also play a crucial role in helping China develop a new generation of military equipment in the future."

Working Hard for China's Car Industry

Ni Jun once said, "Young people are inspired by dreams." Looking calm and composed, he exemplified this statement, having done many "unprecedented" things on impulse.

In 2012, 2016 and 2017, Ni Jun took his team to Germany to participate in the world's top-ranked competition, where their Chinese fuel-powered, electric-powered and driverless racing cars made their international debut. In 2017, he led a team to develop the world's first driverless racing car. He also coordinated with the China Society of Automotive Engineers to establish the Chinese College Students Driverless Car Racing Competition in which he was responsible for formulating the competition rules and was event operator.

Just as he'd said, young people had an obsession to be the best.

"While we were developing our driverless racing car, we heard that other countries were also doing this," Ni Jun said. "We strove to be No. 1 so that the first driverless racing car would be Chinese. We raced against the clock day and night and finally succeeded in developing the first driverless racing car. Actually, everyone on our team has this characteristic: to sacrifice whatever we have to pursue our belief, and we won't hesitate when it's for the good of our country."

According to Ni Jun, being young means having strong beliefs and drive. Being twenty-something, he did something remarkable. Two years ago, he went to Mohe, Heilongjiang Province for a competition on military unmanned vehicles. His team had developed such an unmanned vehicle, and he had to drive to the site to deliver a big lithium cobalt battery with a peak power of 300kw and a 40C ultra-high discharge rate. Alone, he drove through heavy fog and limited visibility to the competition site.

"This battery was very dangerous, so I didn't dare to hand it over to any transportation agency. I rented a business car, took out the back seat, loaded this 300 kilogram 'bomb' into the car and drove 7,000 km from Beijing to Mohe. It took me six days."

"Because I knew my family would worry, I didn't tell them what I was doing. At that time, the Daxinganling Mountains were drenched in fog with bad, rugged roads. If something went wrong with the battery, it could have killed me. When I recalled it now, all that fear came back to me."

Keeping Forging Ahead to Achieve His Dream

Ni Jun believed it was necessary and worthwhile to take one's academic achievements and convert them into industrial applications, so as to facilitate our country's economic growth.

"Academic achievements are usually realized on paper, but I wanted to make these achievements become tangible through industrial applications to truly help boost the national economy. At the same time, we want to push the boundaries of innovation for BIT students from innovation to entrepreneurship so that more tangible scientific and technological achievements can be scored."

In February 2018, Ni Jun and his team launched the "Zhongyun Smart Vehicle" project in which they applied the experience and expertise they learned from the racing car field to the R&D, production, and operation of driverless cars in specific scenarios. They presently have a full line of small, general-purpose vehicles. They've also had a series of notable achievements with their Zhongyun 1.0 chassis, which made its debut at the Beijing International Automotive Exhibition, the World Smart Car Challenge, and other exhibitions. They also won the aforementioned 4th China College Students' Internet Innovation and Entrepreneurship Competition.

For this project, the team created a new model for the R&D and production of driverless vehicles with a focus on developing vehicles for driverless commuting, shipping and military applications. The team has already established strategic partnerships with many e-commerce platforms and large industrial parks. They have also completed the construction of a production base with an expected annual vehicle output capacity of more than 1,200 units.

Since he won the 2018 award, Ni Jun has been thrust into the media spotlight. However, he believed that this award belonged to every teacher who had ever helped him and to every student who had fought by his side over the seven years leading up to the competition. He hoped to continue his research on driverless vehicles after receiving his doctoral degree and to develop the "Zhongyun Smart Vehicle" into a BIT industrial project. He said that he would like to focus on how to integrate the driverless car industry with research and university education, and planned to spend his lifetime on the development of China's smart car industry.

"Do good things, and don't worry about the future." This was how Ni Jun looked forward to the days ahead.

在无声的世界里舞蹈

Dancing in a Silent World

作者：孙惠贤 吴蕴聪
翻译：吴爱俊

在无声的世界里舞蹈

伴随着音乐的律动,舞台上的女孩翩翩起舞,白色的舞裙随着曼妙的舞姿散成花朵的模样。在王力宏《无声感情》的MV里,女主角蒋馨柔举手投足间的优雅和灿烂的笑容,让越来越多的人认识并记住了这个独特的女孩。

蒋馨柔是一名听障女孩,对这个12岁就远离家乡西安来北京追求舞蹈梦的女孩来说,听觉障碍让她付出了更多的艰辛,追梦为她的生命赋予了更多意义。

1994年,刚出生8个月的蒋馨柔还没来得及多倾听一下这个世界的声音,一场突如其来的病毒性湿疹就让她的右耳永久地失去了听力,左耳需借助助听器才能听清。短暂的茫然和无助后,蒋馨柔的妈妈王芸认为,女儿的人生不应该因为医学上的定义而残缺。

在母亲眼里,女儿和别人家的孩子没有

差别。蒋馨柔的声音世界是通过感知震动建立起来的，为了让女儿拥有正常人的生活，能够更好地和同学朋友交流，王芸从没有想过让蒋馨柔学习手语，也没有送女儿上过一天特殊教育学校。蒋馨柔说："我一直和普通孩子一样在学校读书。从小妈妈就教我学习唇语。妈妈会把我的手放在她的颈部，让我感受喉咙的震动和气流发出的声音，并学习模仿。"

为了帮助蒋馨柔发出"喝"的字音，王芸将一口水含在嘴里，通过发声让女儿观察水在嘴里的震动，并让蒋馨柔也含一口水体验。"一开始的时候，因为学不会，我总是把水咽下去。后来妈妈让我含盐水来练习，慢慢地就忍住了。"单是这一个"喝"字，妈妈就教了她三四个月。

没有人告诉王芸应该如何帮助听障的女儿学会发音和说话，在一次次失败和经验积累中，王芸就是这样一个单字一个单字地教会女儿发出声音。蒋馨柔渐渐读懂妈妈的口型，学会了说话和读唇语。

为了帮助女儿找到人生的另一种可能，

王芸开始发掘女儿的兴趣所在。"我本想培养她的绘画兴趣,却发现蒋馨柔似乎在舞蹈方面更有悟性和天赋。"

在舞蹈上,蒋馨柔也逐渐发现了更好的自己。"我从小身体就特别灵活,而且平衡感特别好,我也希望能够将舞蹈作为一个可以毕生付出的事业。"

面对年幼女儿的选择,王芸在一片质疑声中决定支持。蒋馨柔12岁那年,王芸辞去工作,带着女儿到北京学习舞蹈,她的丈夫留在西安经营一间小工厂来支撑全家的开支。"那是我第一次离家,当我在火车上看着站台上爸爸渐渐远去的身影,想到面对未知的恐惧和紧张,我哭了。"此后的十几年,这个幸福的三口之家在两座相距1200公里的城市共同奋斗,父母为女儿的梦想筑起了最坚强的后盾。

得知北京舞蹈学院附属中学以建校以来从未招收过残疾儿童为由拒绝蒋馨柔时,王芸"没想过放弃,也不能放弃"。在王芸的坚持下,校方终于同意让蒋馨柔试读3个月。

虽然有听力障碍,蒋馨柔的模仿能力却

极强。其他同学通过声音理解老师强调的重点，蒋馨柔依靠一次次的模仿感知音律和舞步。"她需要一遍遍观察、模仿掌握动作技巧，再通过反复的课上练习、课下练习熟悉动作要领。"专业课老师郑洁说，对于无声世界里的舞者来说，每完成一支独舞都是一个艰难的过程。

3个月很快就过去了，蒋馨柔迅速融入学校的学习生活，凭借努力和天赋成为正式学生。在老师郑洁看来，蒋馨柔听不见的缺陷恰恰帮助她在舞台上更好地表达出她自己对舞蹈的理解，"虽然蒋馨柔听不到音乐的准确节奏，但是她舞蹈的质感非常好，她是带着心中对舞蹈的纯粹情感去跳的。"正是因为对舞蹈有独特的感知，蒋馨柔的舞蹈才会迸发出更强的感染力和生命力。

在北京舞蹈学院附中学习的日子，蒋馨柔很努力，妈妈王芸也丝毫不敢松懈。为了蒋馨柔能够更好地把握节奏，王芸陪着女儿学习架子鼓。为了帮助女儿理解一曲舞蹈的含义，王芸反复琢磨、耐心地讲解，并把舞步背得滚瓜烂熟……

蒋馨柔跳了6年，王芸陪了6年。终于，蒋馨柔在2012年迎来了高考。

舞蹈《花儿为什么这样红》是蒋馨柔专门为民间舞专业考试准备的。在助听器的帮助下，蒋馨柔只能听到音乐开始的第一声和最后一声，其他动作全靠数拍子完成。"每次表演，我都必须将一整支舞蹈的拍子熟记于心。"备考期间，蒋馨柔每天都和母亲待在北京舞蹈学院附属中学的排练室内，反复练习如何把握正确的开始时间。回到家后，母女俩又坐在一起观看舞蹈视频。"馨柔没办法判断是否跟上节奏，所以我就牢记住每一个舞蹈动作所对应的节奏，面对馨柔跟着视频节奏数节拍，一遍又一遍，让她感受节奏的同时不断重复记忆。"通过努力，蒋馨柔参加了全国高考，并如愿成为北京舞蹈学院2012级民族舞蹈专业的一名本科生。

王芸让女儿始终相信，付出就会有回报。2014年，北京舞蹈学院建校60周年校庆，蒋馨柔眼里的美好世界第一次出现了裂痕。

"舞院排练任务是'恐怖'的。除了正式课程，没有休息的时间，没有吃饭的时间，只有换教室的时间。"2014年9月12日，蒋馨柔在个人微博上记录下了为校庆准备彩排的日常。为了这次校庆，蒋馨柔拿出准备了两年的热巴舞，并参与了七八个舞蹈的排练。在将近4个月里，她每天早上6点睁眼，忙到晚上10点多，拎着各式各样的服装和道具，穿梭于各个舞蹈教室。在王芸看来，这不仅是女儿对校庆表演的重视，更是每一次舞蹈排练的常态。"她总是希望能够尽自己最大的努力，完成每一次舞蹈的呈现。"

距离校庆表演还有4天的时候，意外出现了。在一场群舞的排练过程中，两个本应托举并抛起蒋馨柔的男生因为失误不小心松手，导致蒋馨柔被狠狠摔在地板上，左胳膊错位，完全不能动弹。"我的热巴舞怎么办呀！"无力地瘫趴在地上的蒋馨柔仍然惦记着4天后的演出。

"七八个节目排练同时停止，准备了两年的热巴舞也被迫搁浅。"现在谈起这些，蒋馨柔的神情中依旧透露着些许失落。"为了让我认识这个世界的美好，妈妈总是教导我有付出就会有回报。而这次的失利也让我明白，过程带给我的收获同样非常重要。"

"我可以放弃选择，但是我不能选择放弃，所以坚强是我唯一的选择。"这次失利也让蒋馨柔展现出和母亲一样的坚强与执着。

2016年大学毕业，蒋馨柔没有一个正式、稳定的工作，因为一般的舞蹈团不愿意接收听障人士——哪怕蒋馨柔是北京舞蹈学院建院60年来招收的唯一一个听障生，并且顺利毕业。但蒋馨柔的人生从来都充满希望。大学毕业后，她成为一名自由舞者，还是平面模特和摄影师。

2016年年底，歌星王力宏在参加某综艺节目时结识蒋馨柔，并被她的成长故事感动。在王力宏眼里，蒋馨柔是舞蹈家，是一个能够把个人缺陷变成优点的与众不同的女孩。2017年10月13日，王力宏为蒋馨柔量身定做的歌曲《无声感情》正式发行，蒋馨柔作为歌曲MV的女主角走进了大众的视野。

蒋馨柔终于走上了自己人生舞台的中央，一路支持着女儿成长的王芸除了欣慰，更多的是感激。王芸总是义务反顾地支持女儿的选择，甚至包括支持女儿放弃重获听力的一次机会。

电子耳蜗是一种模拟人类耳蜗毛细胞工作原理的电子植入体。它可以帮助听力损失患者"重获新声"，走进有声世界。蒋馨柔12岁那年，遇到一次能够通过电子耳蜗重获听力的机会。那时的电子耳蜗外部接收器是体携式的，会有根线夹在头发上一直连到腰部的接收器盒子，这会影响跳舞。恢复听力和舞蹈之间，蒋馨柔选择了舞蹈，"我的求学之路来之不易，我没有办法放弃舞蹈"。

在蒋馨柔看来，自己是一个很普通的女孩，她喜欢旅游，喜欢冲浪，也热爱滑雪……她的生活丰富多彩，而她也坚信自己有能力变得更好。她说："有机会我会通过我自己的努力去做手术，我不会再让爸妈为我支付昂贵的手术费，现在应该是我孝敬他们的时候了。"

青春、活力、自信永远洋溢在这个90后女孩的脸上。社交软件上，很多人会私信问她：听不见音乐却选择跳舞，怎么能坚持这么久？坚持这么久是为了什么？每次她都会回答：因为热爱，热爱的东西就不会放弃。

"我要用自己的生命跳出一曲华美的舞蹈，我脚下的道路从来没有停止过，生活这趟远航我不会缺席。"蒋馨柔相信，想去的地方终会抵达。

Dancing in a Silent World

In Wang Leehom's music video "Silent Dancer", performer Jiang Xinrou dances gracefully on the stage, with her white skirt spreading out like flowers. Her graceful gestures and beautiful smile are impossible to forget, and even more unforgettable is the fact that she is deaf.

When she was just 12 years old, she left Xi'an for Beijing to pursue her dream to learn dancing. Her hearing impairment created many hardships for her, but through chasing this dream, it also gave her life more meaning.

In 1994, when she was just eight months old and without enough time to listen to the sounds of the world, she contracted a viral eczema which caused her to permanently lose hearing in her right ear, and her left ear needed a hearing aid. After a period of helplessness and frustration, her mother Wang Yun was convinced that her daughter's life would not be crippled by her condition.

In the eyes of her mother, there is no difference between her daughter and that of another family. Jiang Xinrou "listens" to the world by feeling sound vibrations. In order to help her daughter have a relatively normal life and communicate with her classmates, Wang Yun never insisted her daughter learn sign language, nor did she consider sending her to a special education school. "I studied at school just like ordinary kids," Jiang Xinrou said. "When I was young, my mother taught me how to read lips and also how to speak. She would ask me to touch her neck to feel the vibrations of her throat while speaking and I would imitate this."

In order to help Jiang pronounce the word "drink," Wang Yun kept a mouthful of water in her mouth and asked her daughter to observe how the water vibrated while she spoke. Then she asked Jiang to hold some water in her mouth to also experience it. "At the outset, I always swallowed the water. Then my mother told me to practice with salt water, so I wouldn't drink it, and I slowly held back and gradually got accustomed to it." It took three or four months for her to learn this one character.

No one taught Wang Yun how to teach her deaf daughter to pronounce characters and speak. Although she encountered numerous failures, she was determined to teach her how to speak, pronouncing each character. Jiang gradually could understand her mother by reading her lips, and was eventually able to speak and understand others.

In order to help her daughter discover what she'd like to do in life, Wang Yun began to explore her interest. "I had thought of cultivating her interest in painting, but later I found that she seemed to be more talented in dancing."

Through dancing, Jiang Xinrou gradually discovered her inner strength. "I've always been very flexible since I was young with a good sense of balance. I hope I can devote my entire life to dancing."

Dancing in a Silent World
在无声的世界里舞蹈

Wang Yun decided to support her daughter's decision to dance despite the skepticism of others. When Jiang was just 12 years old, Wang Yun quit her job and took her daughter to Beijing to learn dancing. Jiang's father still stayed in Xi'an to run a small factory to support the family. "It was the first time for me to leave my hometown. Sitting on the train thinking of the unknown future and watching my father walk away on the platform, I burst into tears." Over the next a dozen years, the family worked hard in the two cities, 1,200 kilometers apart. "My parents did everything they could to help me realize my dream."

Upon learning that Jiang's application to the Affiliated Secondary School of Beijing Dance Academy was rejected due to her disability, Wang Yun did not give up. Because of Wang's persistence, the school finally agreed that Jiang could study for a three-month trial period.

Despite her impaired hearing, Jiang had an exceptional ability to imitate. The other students understood the key points by listening to the teacher's words, but Jiang relied on imitation to sense the rhythm and dance steps. Her teacher Zheng Jie remembered, "She needed to observe, imitate, and familiarize with the moves over and over again, and then practice the moves repeatedly in and out of class." She added that in a world of silence, a solo dance was particularly challenging.

The three months flew by. Jiang quickly fitted into school life and became a registered student by her efforts and talent. In the eyes of her teacher, "Jiang's audio defect actually helps her better express her understanding of dance because she dances for pure love of the art." It was her unique perception of dance that enabled Jiang to display stronger emotion and vitality.

While Jiang practiced dancing, her mother also never relaxed. In order to help Jiang improve her rhythm, Wang Yun would accompany her daughter to learn drumming. Also, in order to help her daughter better understand the meaning of a dance piece, Wang Yun would learn each dance and memorize all the steps herself in order to explain the dance to her daughter.

Wang Yun worked with her daughter to learn dancing for six years. In 2012, Jiang took the national college entrance examination.

For her dancing examination, Jiang prepared a dance to the Chinese folk song "Why Are Flowers So Red?" With the help of a hearing aid, Jiang could only hear the first and final note of the music, so she had to count the beats while dancing. "I had to memorize the beats of the entire piece." During her preparation, Jiang and her mother came to the school rehearsal room every day where she practiced over and over again. After returning home, they'd watch the video together, and her mother would count out the beats while facing Jiang as Jiang watched the video, which helped her to memorize the beats and moves. She took the national examination, and later her exam results were announced. Their efforts had paid off. She'd been accepted into the Beijing Dance Academy.

Wang Yun had always told her daughter that hard work would always pay off. But in 2014, on the 60th anniversary of the establishment of the Beijing Dance Academy, something happened that would darken the world in Jiang's eyes for the first time.

"The rehearsal schedules were 'intimidating'. There were no meal or break times between courses," Jiang wrote in her Weibo microblog.

Dancing in a Silent World
在无声的世界里舞蹈

For the school anniversary celebration, Jiang was going to perform the Reba dance which she had been practicing for two years, and would participate in seven or eight other dances. For nearly four months, she got up at 6 o'clock and wouldn't go home until after 10 o'clock at night, carrying all kinds of costumes and props, and shuffling between different dance classrooms. For Wang Yun, this was her daughter's normal routine. The mother said, "She always strove to give her best performance in every presentation."

Four days before the celebration performance, she was rehearsing a group dance. She was lifted up and thrown into the air, and the two boy dancers who were supposed to catch her made a mistake, and Jiang fell to the ground, disjointing her left arm and leaving her unable to move. As she lay in pain on the floor, all she could think was, "So how am I going to do the Reba dance, now?"

"I had to drop out of the seven or eight dances and also the Reba dance," said Jiang, still feeling disappointed. "In order to let me see the beauty of this world, my mother would always tell me that efforts will pay off. But this failure made me realize that process is also important."

"I can give up my choice, but I cannot choose to give up. Perseverance is my only choice." This setback brought out Jiang's strong tenacity, the tenacity just like her mother's.

Upon graduation in 2016, she couldn't find a regular job as dance troupes did not normally recruit hearing impaired dancers, even though Jiang was the only deaf student ever to be enrolled at the Beijing Dance Academy since it was established 60 years ago. But Jiang was still full of hope. After graduation, she became a freelance dancer, graphic model, and photographer.

At the end of 2016, Chinese pop star Wang Leehom met Jiang Xinrou while participating in a variety show, and was greatly moved by her story. He saw her as an artist and a unique girl who had turned her shortcoming into a strength. Wang wrote a song about her called "Silent Dancer," the music video of which premiered on October 13, 2017, and featured Jiang dancing throughout the video. From that moment on, everyone knew the name Jiang Xinrou.

Seeing the recognition for her daughter made her mother feel gratified. Wang Yun had never hesitated to support her daughter, even when Jiang had chosen to abandon an opportunity to regain her hearing.

When she was 12 years old, she had the opportunity to receive a cochlear implant. The implant is an electronic device which simulates the working function of the hair cells in the ear, and can help people regain their hearing. At that time, the external receiver was fixed at the waist, and was connected by a long wire to another device attached to the head. Having this would make it very difficult for her to dance, so Jiang chose not to have it, and to dance instead. "My journey to school was hard-won, and I cannot give up dancing," she recalled.

In Jiang's opinion, she thinks she is just an ordinary girl. She likes traveling, surfing and skiing. Her life is rich and colorful, and she also firmly believes that her life will get better. "I hope to earn enough money to afford the operation costs instead of my parents. Now it's the time for me to show how much I honor them."

This girl born in the 1990s is constantly beaming with youth, vitality and confidence. On social media, many people asked her, "Though you cannot hear music, why do you choose to dance and keep doing it for so long?"

Her reply was the same every time. "Because of my love, I never abandon what I love."

Jiang Xinrou believes that she can go as far in life as she wants. "I want my life to be a gorgeous dance. The road under my feet will never end. I will not be absent from this voyage of life."

Born in the 90s: Never Regretting Our Youth
出彩 90 后：我的青春不后悔

Scan for a Video

用诗歌让乡村孩子感受爱与美

Poetry Helps Rural Children Enjoy Love and Beauty

作者：尹海月
翻译：韩芙芸

用诗歌让乡村孩子感受爱与美

"老师,如果你是礁石就好了,那我们可以变成海浪去拥抱你,可你是天上的星星,我们抱不到你。"

2017年7月,康瑜与陪伴了两年的山区孩子们告别。支教的两年中,她教会他们写诗。离开的那天下着大雨,她在日记里写道:不知道我和老天谁哭得更凶一点。

支教结束,康瑜原本计划出国留学。但两个月后,她以一名公益创业者的身份回来了,公益机构名为"是光",产品是将四季诗歌课程普及到更多乡村学校。

一年多的时间里,康瑜如同一个旋转的陀螺,忙于搭建团队、筹集资金、编写诗歌教材。她每周跑三四个城市,每天睡眠不足6个小时,没有假期,没有收入。

如今,这套诗歌教材已经在云南、山东、河南、甘肃等地的297所中小学使用,覆盖2.6万多名乡村儿童。作为一名经济专业的

Poetry Helps Rural Children Enjoy Love and Beauty
用诗歌让乡村孩子感受爱与美

女生,她本人并不写诗,却为云南省昌宁县漭水镇的孩子们带去了第一堂诗歌课。

2015年,正在中国人民大学经济学院读大四的康瑜放弃保研机会,去云南支教两年。从县城到漭水镇要坐两个多小时的大巴车。由于气候湿热,康瑜很不适应,得了荨麻疹,足足半年才好。她每次家访都要翻山越岭,徒步二三十公里,"腿酸,皮靴都裂开了"。那时她常跟朋友说:"前一段我觉得特别难熬,但是现在都好了。"

相比生活上的波折,康瑜更愿意分享教学过程中的故事和喜悦。

在学校,康瑜教政治和书法。她还每天用两个小时给成绩落后的学生补习,举办"校园十佳歌手"比赛,制作"心思盒"(收到近2000张小纸条)……面对山区孩子闭塞的成长环境和生活苦恼,康瑜一直在寻找更多的方式来拓宽孩子们的视野,打开通往他们心中的门。

一次书法课,天突然下起了大雨,孩子们不约而同地向窗外看。看着入神听雨的孩子们,康瑜当即决定带着他们看雨写诗。"他们听了很吃惊。"康瑜说，面对新生事物，山里的孩子总是怯生生的。

课堂上，有个小女孩吧嗒吧嗒掉眼泪，康瑜过去摸摸她的头，发现她写道：我是一个自私的孩子，我希望雨后的太阳只照射在我一个人身上，温暖我。我是一个自私的孩子，我希望世界上有个角落，能在我伤心的时候空着，安慰我。我是一个自私的孩子，我希望妈妈的爱属于我。

"小女孩写的诗让人心疼。"康瑜想，让孩子们把内心无处诉说的情感通过诗歌表达出来，对他们会不会更好一点儿？

孩子与诗歌似乎有着某种天然契合，二者相遇，会迸发出瑰丽的想象力。他们用"我愿和你自由地好着，像风和风，云和云"来传达对喜欢的人的情意；用"天高万丈，山是一半"来寄托对在外打工的父亲的思念；用"夜晚到清晨，时间慢吞吞"来形容失眠的情绪。

康瑜说，山里的孩子多是留守儿童，家庭养育缺失，他们最需要的是陪伴与关注。看见自信又活泼的城市小孩，她很感慨。相

Poetry Helps Rural Children Enjoy Love and Beauty
用诗歌让乡村孩子感受爱与美

比之下，乡村孩子多数自卑，面对表扬，他们不是说"谢谢"，而是本能地跑掉、躲开。他们对康瑜说："老师，你只是因为偏心我们，才会看我们哪儿都好，为什么没有别人夸我们？"

对大山里的孩子而言，如果没有光亮，人生就会越来越往下掉。康瑜觉得，那束光就是诗歌。

"我觉得我很漂亮，我比蝴蝶漂亮；我觉得我很聪明，我比班长聪明。为什么我漂亮聪明，因为我是最独特的。"有一位小女孩这样写道。康瑜希望诗歌能使山里的孩子获得这样的自信，认识到自我的价值。

在孩子们所写的诗歌里，康瑜最喜欢的是这首《星河》：黑色的夜晚星星在闪耀，我在河边无忧无虑地散步，当我回头看我身边的河水时，只见无数的星星在河里流动。

实际上，山里环境没那么好，夜里蚊虫很多，"能写出这样的诗歌，内心一定是强大的，能够体察生活之美的"。这正是康瑜希望诗歌传达给孩子们的生活态度——从困顿的生活里看到美好的东西，获得生活的力量。

这也是漭水初级中学校长于春云的理念，"我不企求能培养出多少诗人，只想让我的每个学生能走上正常的人生轨道"。

自从初一开设诗歌课以来，于春云发现，初一的孩子们比其他年级的孩子变化更明显：不逃学了，违纪情况大幅减少，语言行为更规范，连砸玻璃的现象也少了很多。会写诗的孩子不砸玻璃——这句话后来成为"是光"的品牌口号。

于春云告诉康瑜，最需要关注的是后进生，"好学生最后都会去大城市，剩在乡村里的就是这批后进生，他们如何，未来的乡村就如何"。

这句话影响和指导了康瑜的乡村教育实践。"是光"选择陪伴的正是那些可能留在山村里的孩子，以此来改变中国乡村的面貌。"当一个孩子观察这个世界的内在视角发生改变，未来才会有更多的力量改变外部世界。"

在讲述自己的公益历程时，康瑜常常提到自己的奶奶。奶奶出身大户人家，嫁给了做农民的爷爷。因为不会劳作，她就在田埂上给农民们讲故事,农民们帮她干活儿。在特别差的环境里,奶奶唱歌,观察花,可以跟周围所有的东西对话。这给了康瑜启示——被苦难包围的人如何有力量地生活。

"我们的世界需要奶奶这样的人,他们的存在让别人过得更好。"康瑜一直在沿着这个轨迹努力向前。

康瑜很喜欢《牧羊少年奇幻之旅》这本书,书里说,每个人都有自己的天命,当意识到自己的天命时,生命的所有意义就实现了。康瑜觉得,投身于乡村诗歌教育就是她的天命。

康瑜离开漭水后,孩子们偷偷往她以前住所的门缝里塞纸条,支教的队友收集了一整箱,寄给康瑜。有个小女孩写道:康老师,我希望有更多的孩子像我一样,在诗歌中找到自己。这句话使康瑜下决心不再出国,留下来做公益。

康瑜再次回到了大山,而且为孩子们带去了更多的"康老师"。"是光"课程开发团队成员来自清华大学、中国人民大学、武汉大学、浙江大学、华盛顿大学等名校。

"是光"四季诗歌课程参考了语文课标、儿童心理学、现代诗歌体系，并根据不同年级、不同季节设计具体教学内容。申请诗歌课需要学校里农村的孩子达到70%以上，通常，这些学校位置偏远，资源缺乏，缺少关注。

山东省临朐县寺头镇李季小学是一处乡村教学点，地理位置偏僻，师资力量薄弱。2017年冬天，学校的支教老师申请"是光"四季诗歌课程后，康瑜坐了一夜火车去看望那里的孩子。孩子们脸冻得通红，正在读一首关于春天的诗：春天是一匹世界上最美丽的彩布，燕子是个卖布郎，他随身带着一把剪刀，每天忙忙碌碌地东飞飞西剪剪……康瑜至今仍然记得那个场景，并深深地为之感动。

通过申请后，课程的教材和培训都将免费提供。每个孩子平均花费25元，课程的开发、制作和邮递，一切费用都由机构承担。她建了一个打卡群，老师们每天将学生们的诗歌上传，被评获奖的孩子会收到80元稿费和特意塑封过的奖状。

"是光"的运转需要资金支持。康瑜的母亲每次跟她聊天，问的第一句都是"身体好不好，还有没有钱"。康瑜动用了一部分出国留学的费用。目前，机构已经获得几家基金会、企业和个人的捐赠，但只够一半的运营费用。

张田田在一场公益活动上认识康瑜后，辞职加入"是光"。2018年10月，她们将第一次领取工资。除了两位全职人员，"是光"还有49名长期核心志愿者，以及750多名活跃志愿者。

康瑜说，很多人对公益存在误解，好像做公益的人就不该拿工资，全部的资金都要拿去做好事。对此，她显得有些无奈。

在公益组织建立初期，如果没有一定的规模，想要得到关注和资金支持非常困难。康瑜也听到过怀疑的声音，认为她在以此博取名利。康瑜希望将更多的精力放在诗歌产品的升级和项目实实在在的落地上，"让'是光'的每一步都走得扎实"。

诗人朵渔担任诗歌产品内容设计的顾问。他说，康瑜非常符合他理想中的公益人形象：热情，能干，行动力强，有感染力，有一种为理想去奋斗的劲头。

一次，康瑜和伙伴一起去大山里拍摄一部公益纪录片，片子的主人公是一个身体患有疾病的小男孩，他在诗歌课上写星空、宇宙、星球，梦想是做一名宇航员。"是光"看到他诗里的心愿，给他寄去一个关于宇宙的绘本。他回家后开始愿意讲学校里的事情，"老师表扬了我。"他跟家里人说，他觉得自己跟别的小朋友不一样。

这样的故事给康瑜带来了力量。

"不是所有的老师都喜欢教诗歌"，康瑜希望乡村教师能通过诗歌获得幸福感，再充满热情地教学。

在某些时刻，她也曾经脆弱。去督查项目落地情况时，常要坐夜车去偏远山区，康瑜跟朋友说，每次坐车心里都会害怕。但在公共视野里，她像一个战士，从未停止过奋斗。

康瑜认为自己做的不是一份领着薪水、养家糊口的工作，而是一种使命，一项实现自我价值的事业。这与她的个人生活并不冲突,"别人会说我放弃这个放弃那个,我觉得这样的描述不好,我很清楚自己在做什么,不是放弃,是选择"。

Poetry Helps Rural Children Enjoy Love and Beauty

"Teacher, if you are a rock, then we can turn into waves to hug you, but you are a star in the sky, so we cannot hug you."

In July 2017, Kang Yu said goodbye to the children in the mountainous area who had been with her for two years. During her two years as a volunteer teacher, she taught them how to write poems. It was raining heavily on the day she left, she wrote in her diary: I don't know who cried harder, me or heaven.

After finishing teaching, Kang Yu had planned to study abroad. But two months later, she returned as a social entrepreneur. Her organization was named "Being the Light," and it aimed to bring Four Seasons Poetry to more rural schools.

For more than a year, Kang Yu was busy forming teams, raising money, and compiling poetry textbooks like a spinning top. She visited three or four cities a week and slept less than six hours a day without vacations or income.

Today, her poetry textbooks have been used in 297 primary and secondary schools in Yunnan, Shandong, Henan, Gansu, and other provinces among more than 26,000 rural children. As an economics major, she does not write poetry, but she gave the first poetry lesson to the children of Mangshui Town in Changning County, Yunnan Province.

In 2015, Kang Yu, a senior at the School of Economics, Renmin University of China, turned down a postgraduate recommendation and went to Yunnan to volunteer for two years. It took more than two hours to take a bus from the county to Mangshui Town. As the climate there was hot and humid, Kang Yu did not get used to it and had hives, from which she recovered fully after half a year. Every time she visited her students' home, she crossed the mountains and walked 20 or 30 kilometers. "My legs were sore, and my boots were cracked," she used to tell her friends. "I felt very hard for a while, but now it's all right."

Compared with the difficulties in life, Kang Yu is more willing to share the stories and joys in her teaching.

At school, Kang Yu taught politics and calligraphy. She also spent two hours a day tutoring students who fell behind, organized the "Top Ten Singers on Campus" competition, and made a "mind box" (with nearly 2,000 small notes)… Seeing the disadvantaged environment and troubles of children's lives in the mountainous area, Kang Yu had been looking for more ways to broaden their horizons and open up their hearts.

In a calligraphy class, it suddenly rained heavily, and the children all looked out of the windows. Seeing the students listening to the rain attentively, Kang Yu immediately decided to take the children to watch the rain and write poems. "They were very surprised to hear that." Kang Yu said that in the face of new things, the children in the mountainous area were always timid.

In a class, a little girl was weeping. Kang Yu went to touch her head and found that she wrote: I am a selfish child. I hope the sun after the rain only shines on me and warms me. I am a selfish child. I hope there is a corner in the world, being empty when I am sad, and can comfort me. I am a selfish child. I want my mother to love me only.

"The poem written by the little girl hurts." Kang Yu thought if it would be better for children to express their feelings through poetry.

Children and poetry seemed to have a natural fit. When they met, it would burst out magnificent imagination. They would use "I would like to be close friends freely with you, like wind with wind, cloud with cloud" to convey their feelings for those they like. They would use "The sky is ten thousand feet high, the mountain is half" to express their yearning for their fathers, who worked outside. They would use "From night to early morning, time is so slow" to describe their insomnia.

Kang Yu said that most of the children in the mountain area were left-behind children, lacked a proper family upbringing, and what they needed most were companionship and attention. Having seen the confident and lively urban children, she felt emotional. In contrast, most rural children felt inferior. They did not say "thank you" in the face of praise, but would instinctively run away. They said to Kang Yu, "Teacher, it is only because you like us that you think we are all good. Why hasn't anyone else praised us?"

For the children in the mountainous area, if there is no light, life will fall down and down. Kang Yu felt that the beam of light was poetry.

One little girl wrote: "I think I am very beautiful, more beautiful than the butterfly; I think I am very smart, smarter than our monitor. Why am I beautiful and smart? Because I am unique." Kang Yu hoped that poetry could make these children gain such self-confidence and realize their self-worth.

Among the poems written by the children, Kang Yu's favorite was the piece named "River of Stars": The stars were shining in the dark night. I walked carefreely by the river. When I looked back at the river beside me, I saw countless stars flowing in the river.

The environment was not so poetic in the mountain. There were many mosquitoes at night. "If a child can write such a poem, his/her heart must be strong and can observe the beauty of life." This was precisely the attitude towards life that Kang Yu hoped to convey to children in the poems — looking for the good things from a hard life to gain strength in life.

This was also the concept of Yu Chunyun, the principal of Mangshui Junior Secondary School, "I don't expect to train many poets, but I just want every student of mine to embark on a normal life track."

Since offering poetry classes in the first grade of her school, Yu Chunyun has found that the children have changed more obviously than those in other grades: they did not play truant; the number of violations of discipline had been significantly reduced; their language became more standardized and they behaved better; even the disciplinary offense of smashing windows became much less. Children who can write poetry don't break windows, which later became the brand slogan of "Being the Light".

Yu Chunyun told Kang Yu to pay close attention to the underachievers. "Good students will eventually go to the big cities, and the underachievers will be left in the countryside. The countryside's future will depend on them."

This had influenced and guided Kang Yu's rural education practice. "Being the Light" chose to accompany just those who might stay in the mountainous villages, which helped change the Chinese countryside. "When a child's inner perspective of observing the world changes, he/she will have more power to change the outside world in the future."

When discussing her public welfare career, Kang Yu often mentioned her grandmother, born in a rich and influential family, and married her grandfather, a farmer. Because she did not know how to work in the field, she would sit on the ridge to tell stories to the farmers while they helped her with the farm work. In an awful environment, her grandma sang, observed flowers, and would talk to everything around her. This gave Kang Yu inspiration on how to live with strength when sufferings surround you.

"Our world needs people like my grandma, whose existence makes others live a better life." Kang Yu had been working hard along this track.

Kang Yu likes the book *Alquimista* very much. It says in the book that everyone has their own destinies, and when they realize their destinies, all the meanings of life are realized. Kang Yu felt that it was her destiny to devote herself to rural poetry education.

After Kang Yu left Mangshui, the children secretly stuffed notes into the crack of the door of her former residence, and her teammates collected a whole box and sent it to Kang Yu. A little girl wrote: Teacher Kang, I hope more children like me find themselves in poetry. These words made Kang Yu determined not to go abroad and stay to start a social enterprise.

Kang Yu returned to the mountainous village again and brought more "Teacher Kang" to the children. The Being the Light curriculum development team members come from famous universities, such as Tsinghua University, Renmin University of China, Wuhan University, Zhejiang University, University of Washington, etc.

Four Seasons Poetry Course provided by Being the Light refers to the curriculum standards of Chinese class, child psychology, and modern poetry system, and designs specific teaching content according to different grades and seasons. More than 70 percent of the children in the schools had to hold rural registered permanent residence to apply for the poetry class. Usually, these schools are located in remote areas and lack resources and attention.

Liji Primary School, located in Sitou Town, Linqu County, Shandong Province, is a rural school with a remote geographical location and less qualified teachers. In the winter of 2017, Kang Yu took a night train to visit the children after the school's volunteer teachers applied for the Four Seasons Poetry Course of "Being the Light". The children's faces were red with cold, and they were reading a poem about spring: Spring is the most beautiful colored cloth in the world. The swallow is a cloth seller, who carries a pair of scissors with him, and is busy cutting here and there every day. Kang Yu still remembered the scene and was deeply moved by it.

After the application was approved, the course textbooks and training would be provided free of charge. The average cost of each child was 25 yuan. And the development, printing, and mailing of the course textbooks were all borne by the organization. She set up a WeChat group for daily attendance, where teachers could upload students' poems every day. The children who won a prize would receive 80 yuan as a reward and a specially laminated certificate of merit.

The operation of "Being the Light" needs funding. Every time Kang Yu's mother chatted with her, the first thing she asked was, "Are you in good health? Do you have money?" Kang Yu used part of the money prepared for her studying abroad. So far, her organization has received donations from several foundations, enterprises, and individuals, but only enough for half of its operation costs.

After meeting Kang Yu at a public welfare event, Zhang Tiantian resigned and joined "Being the Light". In October 2018, they received their first salaries. Apart from the two full-time staff members, "Being the Light" has 49 permanent core volunteers and more than 750 active volunteers.

Kang Yu said that many people had misunderstandings about public welfare, thinking that people who engaged in public welfare should not be paid, and all the funds should be used to do good things. She seemed a little frustrated.

In the early stage of establishment of a public welfare organization, if it does not reach a certain scale, it will be very difficult to draw great attention and get financial support. Kang Yu has also heard voices of suspicion that she is doing this to gain fame and wealth. Kang Yu hoped to put more energy on upgrading its poetry products and the actual implementation of the project, "so that every step of 'Being the Light' is solid."

The poet Duoyu served as a consultant for the content design of poetry products. He said that Kang Yu was very much in line with his ideal image of a public welfare person: enthusiastic, capable, decisive in action, attractive, and having the drive to strive for ideals.

Once, Kang Yu and her partners went to shoot a public welfare documentary in the mountains. The protagonist was a diseased little boy. He wrote about the stars, the universe and the planets in the poetry class. His dream was to become an astronaut. "Being the Light" found the wish in his poem and sent him a cosmic picture book. After he got home, he began to voluntarily talk about what happened at school. "The teacher praised me." He told his family that he felt different from other children.

Such stories brought strength to Kang Yu.

"Not all teachers like to teach poetry," Kang Yu said. She hoped that rural teachers could get happiness through poetry and then teach enthusiastically.

Sometimes she had been vulnerable. When going to supervise the implementation of the project, she used to take the night bus to remote mountainous areas. Kang Yu told friends that every time she felt afraid. But in the eyes of other people, she was like a soldier and never stopped fighting.

Kang Yu believed that what she did was not a paid job to support her family, but a mission and a cause to realize her self-worth, which did not conflict with her personal life. "Others will say that I give up this and that. I don't think that's a good description. I know what I'm doing. It's not giving up, but a choice I've made."

Poetry Helps Rural Children Enjoy Love and Beauty
用诗歌让乡村孩子感受爱与美

Scan for a Video

"北斗"背后的 90 后

The Post-90s Generation Behind BDS

作者：邱晨辉
翻译：韩芙芸

"北斗"背后的90后

得知"北斗"三号号最后一颗全球组网卫星发射成功时,46岁的中国航天科技集团一院总体部主任设计师胡炜向记者感慨道:"这是创新的胜利,也是年轻的胜利,我们就是要永远保持年轻的心态、创新的冲动!"

这位航天"老兵"所在的队伍成功研制出"长三甲"系列火箭,该系列火箭成为中国唯一的"北斗专列"。2000年,"长三甲"系列火箭发射我国第一颗"北斗"导航试验卫星,至2020年共进行了44次"北斗"发射,将全部"北斗"卫星成功护送升空,发射成功率达100%。即便放眼世界航天舞台,这样的成绩也比较罕见。

然而,在"北斗专列"的研制过程中,这支队伍面对的挑战是:既要有稳定的技术状态,又要不断改进提高火箭的适应力和可靠性。这一度被认为是"鱼与熊掌,不可兼得"

的挑战。

为了"鱼与熊掌"兼得，胡炜带领当时平均年龄不足30岁的总体设计团队，仅用几年时间就完成了以多窗口发射技术和复合制导技术为代表的多项技术攻关，攻克了低温火箭运载能力提升、低温加注后长时间停放等研制难题。

改变30年不变的流程

三十出头的朱平平虽然是火箭研制团队里的年轻面孔，但是担任"长三乙"火箭动力系统指挥的他，已经是研制团队的骨干。团队里还流传着他的几则故事。其中一个和火箭加注有关，因为火箭加注的所有环节朱平平都必须在场。

在一次火箭执行北斗任务时，意外突然发生。

数据显示，常规加注量比要求值低了一些。朱平平的神经立即绷紧，他和同事停下手头的活儿，第一时间定位故障、重新计算加注量、讨论解决方法，精准完成了一系列危机处理动作。

等问题解决后,火箭可以准时发射,朱平平却倒在了工作岗位上。

之后,他被确诊为急性肠梗阻。医生告诉小伙子,情况很危急,有的急性肠梗阻发展过快甚至会导致死亡。朱平平听后冒出一身冷汗,在此前完成任务的过程中,他虽然感到腹部疼痛,却总觉得可以忍。

"那时候,确实顾不上那点儿疼痛了。"朱平平说。

和这位90后有关的另一个故事,关键词是"打破传统"。

在点火发射前,"长三乙"火箭需要补加两次推进剂,这样的流程在中国航天领域已经沿用了近30年。朱平平却成功地将两次补加"合二为一",打破了这一传统,改变了这项30年不变的流程。

朱平平告诉记者,以前的"第一次补加"是为了预冷发动机,"第二次补加"则是补充预冷时挥发的推进剂。每一次补加都需要上百条口令,要不断打开、关闭各种阀门。这不仅带来巨大的工作量,还暗藏了一些出错的风险点。

"有没有可能压缩流程呢？"朱平平和同事们大胆设想，让推进剂靠重力作用流入发动机，并适当延长预冷时间，以达到预冷效果，这样就能精简加压、泄压的流程，减少推进剂挥发。

很快，朱平平的设想在地面试验中得到验证。不过，补加环节已经非常临近发射，任何一点儿小失误都可能造成不可挽回的损失，必须反复推敲、反复验证。

"这个事情可不是讲一个故事那么简单，必须考虑到各个层面的因素。比如，推进剂挥发与温度等因素有关。"朱平平说，他和团队就此又开展了多次大型试验。

说白了，他们要做的，就是证明这种方法在不同季节、不同时段、不同温度条件下都能成功——只有这样，新方法才会被认可，这群年轻人才能真正改变30年不变的推进剂补加流程。

如今，"长三甲"系列火箭的发射场工作，周期一步一步缩短，流程一步一步优化：从一开始的50～60天，到现在的20～22天。

这背后就有推进剂补加流程改变的功劳。

"我们的每一步改进都离不开汗水和智慧，更离不开老一辈航天人打下的基础。"朱平平说，为国铸箭是他们这一代航天人的责任，这不仅需要他们继承老一辈航天人严慎细实的作风，还要胆大心细，敢挑重担，有敢于创新的勇气。

跑三个学校投简历，就是要进航天

1994年出生的许哲琪，是"长三甲"系列火箭研制团队里最年轻的队员之一，是一个不折不扣的航天"后浪"。

在成为一名航天人之前，许哲琪对火箭最深的印象就是新闻报道中雷霆万钧、一飞冲天的瞬间。"当时就觉得，这么大的火箭，要飞起来，还要把卫星精准送入轨道，太不容易了。"她说。

她的航天梦想，还要从一次宣讲会说起。

一次偶然的机会，许哲琪听了一场中国运载火箭技术研究院（即中国航天科技集团一院）的宣讲会。航天人一代代接续奋斗的故事让她深受感动和鼓舞，她从此下定决心要成为火箭研制队伍中的一员。

有意思的是，在许哲琪毕业时，火箭院并未在她所读的大学开设宣讲会，于是她跑了三个不同的大学，并在网上投了简历，多路并进，最终才成了航天系统的一员。

入职以后，为了学习与火箭相关的知识，许哲琪下班后会在办公室看看设计图，学习相关文献。那时，她注意到一个现象：几乎每天，老师黄皓都在加班，一定要把当天的工作当天做完才下班，从不拖到第二天。

刚接触综合试验时，许哲琪还没有树立产品把控的概念。在一次接线时，她从线上削下来一段3毫米左右的胶皮。由于胶皮比较小，许哲琪没有及时扔进垃圾桶，随手放在了桌上。

黄皓看见了，突然严肃起来，朝着许哲琪的方向喊道："这是人为制造多余物，桌上很多插孔、插头，这么小的胶皮随手放在桌上，极可能造成堵塞！"

那是许哲琪第一次看见黄皓这么严肃，

小姑娘有些吃惊。在此之前，老师在她心里是个有耐心的航天前辈，如今因为这件"小事"批评自己，她有些委屈，也有些不解。

很快，这位90后反应了过来，"都怪自己对待试验不谨慎，害老师差点儿发了脾气"。这件"小事"也让她意识到，此前新闻报道里常说的"航天人的严谨"，竟离自己如此的近。更重要的是，这份严谨没有那么多的情怀可以渲染，就是日常工作"细致细致再细致"。

"每一次发射成功，都离不开每个人对细节的把控，但凡有一个人粗心大意，都可能将所有人的努力毁于一旦！"许哲琪告诉记者，几年过去，她也逐渐学会了火箭研制人员的严慎细实。

90后站上指挥岗位

这一次发射是许哲琪第一次独立担任测量系统指挥。90后也站上了指挥岗位。

测量系统指挥岗是一个协调统筹的角色，要求担任指挥的人员根据日程工作安排，与相关岗位及技术负责人沟通后发布每天的工作，调动系统人员配合，时刻关注前后端工作情况，向发射队及时汇报。

刚到发射场时，这位小姑娘还是有些紧张。这是她第一次担任指挥岗，又是"北斗"全球组网的最后一次发射，意义重大。她每天必须加班看测试细则和操作规程，她总觉得，自己多熟悉一些细则和规程，就多一份底气。发射队的很多前辈和同事也给她打气，给了她不少帮助。

2020年6月23日9时43分，"长三乙"火箭点火升空。看着屏幕上的发射直播画面，测试间里的许哲琪流下泪水。

在火箭院的研制队伍中，像胡炜那样几十年如一日坚守岗位的人，像朱平平那样敢挑重担、勇攀高峰的人，像许哲琪那样刚走上工作岗位的新人，还有很多。

"'北斗'发射任务持续20年，完成这项庞大的工程，离不开一代代航天人的接续奋斗，离不开航天精神的传承。要问航天精神是如何传承的？就像一线的航天人一样，从前人手中接过火炬，在平凡的岗位上发光发热。""长三乙"火箭发射队临时党委副书记、中国航天科技集团一院团委书记李迪克说。

相比于那些90后航天人，胡炜说自己早已不那么年轻了，不过他依然清晰地记得一位前辈的教诲——

当你感觉每天所做的工作陌生、费解、不懂时，要去问别人、请教别人，这并不可怕，这说明你在进步；但当你对每天干的工作都很熟悉，闭着眼睛都知道怎么干时，这时候就要警惕，因为你很可能是在原地踏步。

"所以，我们不敢懈怠，要像年轻人那样永远年轻，永远创新。"胡炜说。

The Post-90s Generation Behind BDS

When learning of the successful launch of the last global networking satellite of Beidou-3, 46-year-old Hu Wei, chief designer of the General Design Department of China Aerospace Science and Technology Corporation's First Academy, said to the journalist with emotion, "This is a victory of innovation, and also a victory of the youth. We should always maintain a young mentality and an urge to innovate!"

This "veteran" and his space team successfully developed the Long March 3A series of rockets, which became the only "Beidou special express" in China. In 2000, China's first Beidou navigation test satellite was launched onboard this series of rockets. By 2020, 44 Beidou launches had been carried out, successfully sending all Beidou satellites into orbit, with a success rate of 100 percent. Even in the world space arena, such achievements are rare.

However, in developing the Long March 3A rockets, the team faced the challenge of keeping a stable technical state and constantly improving the adaptability and reliability of the rockets, which was once considered a dilemma.

To solve the dilemma, Hu Wei led the general design team with an average age of fewer than 30 years at that time to complete a number of technical research projects including multi-window launching technology and composite guidance technology in only a few years and tackle the development problems of improving the carrying capacity of cryogenic rockets and placing them for a long time after cryogenic filling.

Changing a Process That Has Remained Unchanged for 30 Years

Since Zhu Pingping is in his early thirties, he is fairly young in the rocket development team, but he is already the backbone of the team as the chief of the power system of the Long March 3B rocket. Several of his stories are still told in the team. One of them is related to the rocket filling because Zhu Pingping must be present at all steps of the rocket filling.

Once a rocket was to be launched to carry out the Beidou mission, and an accident happened suddenly.

The data showed that the conventional filling amount was a little lower than required. Zhu Pingping's nerves immediately were strained, and he and his colleagues stopped their work at hand, immediately located the fault, recalculated the amount of filling, discussed solutions, and accurately completed a series of actions to handle the crisis.

After the problem was solved, and the rocket could be launched on time, yet Zhu Pingping collapsed.

Later, he was diagnosed with acute intestinal obstruction. The doctor told the young man that his situation was critical, and some acute intestinal obstruction might develop too fast and even lead to death. After hearing this, Zhu Pingping broke out in a cold sweat. Although he felt abdominal pain at work before, he felt that he could endure it.

"At that time, I really didn't have time to attend to the pain," Zhu Pingping said.

The keyword of another story related to this post-90s young man is "breaking the tradition".

Before ignition and launch, the Long March 3B rocket needed to add propellant twice, which had been a standard practice in China's space industry for nearly 30 years. However, Zhu Pingping succeeded in "combining the two into one", which broke the tradition and changed this 30-year practice.

Zhu Pingping told the journalist that the previous "first adding" was to precool the engine, and the "second adding" was to supplement the volatile propellant during precooling. Each time required hundreds of passwords, and various valves need to be opened and closed constantly, which brought a huge workload and potential risks.

"Is it possible to simplify the process?" Zhu Pingping and his colleagues boldly envisaged that the propellant would flow into the engine by gravity. The precooling time would be extended appropriately to achieve the precooling effect to simplify the process of pressurization and decompression and reduce the volatilization of propellant.

Soon Zhu Pingping's idea was verified in the ground test. However, the propellant adding steps were close to the launch, and any small fault might cause irreparable losses. So they needed repeated deliberation and verification.

"This is not as simple as telling a story. We must take into account factors at all levels, such as propellant volatilization and temperature." Zhu Pingping said that he and his team had carried out many large-scale experiments concerning this.

To put it bluntly, they needed to prove that this method could be successful in different seasons, different periods of time, and temperature conditions. Only in this way could the new method be recognized, and the young people could really change the propellant adding process that has remained unchanged for 30 years.

Today, the time of the launch site work of the Long March 3A series of rockets had been shortened step by step, and the process has been optimized step by step: from 50 to 60 days at the beginning to 20 to 22 days now. Behind this, a change in the process of propellant adding contributed significantly.

"Every step of our improvement is inseparable from our sweat and wisdom, also from the foundation laid by the older generation of aerospace." Zhu Pingping said that making rockets for the country was the responsibility of their generation of aerospace, which required them not only to maintain the strict and meticulous work style of the older generation, but also to be bold and careful, to dare to shoulder heavy burdens, and have the courage to innovate.

Submitting Resume Three Times to Enter the Aerospace Industry

Xu Zheqi, born in 1994, was one of the youngest members of the Long March 3A series rocket development team and an out-and-out new hand of the aerospace industry.

Before entering into the aerospace industry, Xu Zheqi's most profound impression of the rocket was the thunderous and soaring moment in the news report. "At that time, I felt that it was not easy to launch such a big rocket and bring the satellite into orbit accurately," she said.

Her dream of aerospace started with a lecture.

By chance, Xu Zheqi listened to a lecture given by the China Academy of Launch Vehicle Technology (hereafter referred to as CALVT, also called the First Academy of China Aerospace Science and Technology Corporation). She was deeply moved and inspired by the story of the continuous struggle of the people from generation to generation there. She made up her mind to become a member of the rocket development team.

Interestingly, when Xu Zheqi graduated, the Academy did not hold a recruiting lecture at her university, so she had to go to three other universities to submit her resume, send it online, and finally become a member of the aerospace system.

After entering the post, Xu Zheqi would read the design drawings in the office after work and study the relevant articles to learn the knowledge related to rockets. At that time, she noticed that almost every day, Huang Hao, the teacher, was working overtime. He would finish his work of the day before he got off work. He never put it off until the next day.

When she first came into contact with the comprehensive test, Xu Zheqi had not yet had the concept of product control. During wiring, she cut off a piece of rubber about 3 mm from the wire. As the rubber was relatively small, Xu Zheqi did not throw it into the trash can in time instead of putting it on the table.

When Huang Hao saw it, he suddenly became serious and shouted in the direction of Xu Zheqi, "This is an artificial surplus. There are many jacks and plugs on the table. Such a small rubber is casually placed on the table, which is very likely to cause blockage!"

It was the first time that Xu Zheqi found Huang Hao was so serious. The little girl was surprised. Before that, the teacher in her heart was a patient senior, now because of this "trivial matter", he was criticizing her. She felt grieved and puzzled.

Soon, the post-90s reacted, "I blamed myself for not being careful about the experiment, and made the teacher almost lose his temper." This "trivial matter" also made her realize that the "rigor of aerospace people" often mentioned in previous news reports was so close to her. More importantly, this rigor did not have to connect with so many feelings. It only required your daily work to be "meticulous and more".

"Every successful launch cannot be separated from the control of details of everyone. Even if one person is careless, it may ruin the efforts of all people!" Xu Zheqi told the journalist that she had gradually learned the rigor and meticulousness of rocket developers over the past few years.

The Post-90s Taking the Post of Chief

During this launch, Xu Zheqi acted as independent chief of the measuring system for the first time. The post-90s generation began to take the post of chief.

The chief of the measuring system is in charge of coordination and overall planning. The chief should release the daily work after communicating with the relevant posts and technical responsible persons according to the work schedule, mobilize the system personnel to cooperate, pay attention to the front and rear end working conditions and report to the launch team in time.

When she arrived at the launch site, the young woman was a little nervous. This was her first launch at the post of chief and the last launch of the Beidou global network, which was of great significance. She had to work overtime every day to read the test specifications and operating procedures, and she always felt that if she were more familiar with the specifications and procedures, she would have more confidence. Many predecessors and colleagues of the launch team also encouraged her and gave her lots of help.

At 9:43 on June 23, 2020, the Long March 3B rocket was ignited and launched. Looking at the live broadcast of the launch on the screen, Xu Zheqi shed tears in the test room.

In the research and development team of the CALVT, there are many people like Hu Wei who have been sticking to their posts for decades, people like Zhu Pingping who dare to shoulder heavy burdens and scale the peak of science bravely, and newcomers like Xu Zheqi who have just started their career.

"The Beidou launch mission has lasted for 20 years, and the completion of this huge project is inseparable from the continuous struggle of generations of people in the aerospace industry and the inheritance of the aerospace spirit. How is the aerospace spirit passed on? We take the torch from our predecessors and shine in our ordinary posts," said Li Dike, Deputy Secretary of the Provisional Party Committee of the Long March 3B Rocket Launch Team and Secretary of the Youth League Committee of the First Academy of China Aerospace Science and Technology Corporation.

Compared with those post-90s, Hu Wei said that he was not so young, but he still clearly remembered the teachings of a senior:

When the work you do every day is unfamiliar, hard to understand, and you don't know how to do it, you need to ask and consult others; it is not necessarily a bad thing. It shows that you are making progress. But when the work you do every day is familiar, and you know how to do it even with your eyes closed, you should be alert because you are likely to be marking time.

"Therefore, we don't dare to slack off. We should always keep our mind young and innovative like young people," said Hu Wei.

让"红旗"更加招展

Making the Hongqi (Red Flag) Car More Captivating

作者：程鸿鹤
翻译：卢 敏

让"红旗"更加招展

晚上 8 点刚过，李登山不到 15 平方米的单身宿舍挤进两位同事，显得满满当当。他们盯着各自的手机屏幕，或站、或卧，房间里只能听见手机外放的声音。

2020 年 1 月 8 日，红旗 H9 汽车在北京第一次公开亮相，李登山和同事们约好了一起看直播。

"快看快看，快到我们 NVH 的部分了！"李登山一声招呼，两位同事瞬间扭过头。

"哪儿呢哪儿呢，我们看的直播怎么还没到？"因为不同平台直播进度不一，三人都聚集到李登山的手机前，很快又安静下来。他将手机高高举起，手里冒出汗也不敢放下手机，生怕错过了那一瞬间。

"红旗 H9 已实现风噪（17 宋）国际领先水平，路噪（54 分贝）白金水平。"当不到 30 字的红旗 H9NVH 性能信息打在大屏幕上，李登山和身边的同事一下子笑了出来。"看到红旗H9亮相，就像自己的孩子考上了清华，心里特别甜。"

尽管隔着将近1000公里，李登山的心却早已飞到了发布会现场。为了这一天，他已经期待了两年零两个月。

做研发就要找最强对手

NVH是车辆噪音（Noise）、振动（Vibration）和声振粗糙度（Harshness）的简称，被视为汽车品控的一大难点。有数据显示，每辆汽车约有1/3的故障与NVH有关。

"一处异响的背后，可能涉及多个总成单元的调校工作。"李登山告诉记者，在业内，NVH被视为衡量汽车制造品质的重要指标，也是全球汽车品牌和零部件企业关注的重点问题之一。

2016年从大连理工大学毕业后，李登山加入中国第一汽车集团有限公司（以下简称"中国一汽"），担任车身声学包与气密封分析员。随后，红旗品牌迎来前所未有的改革，并树立了新目标。

用这位90后工程师的话说，"自己一入职场就赶上了红旗的历史性时刻"。在李登山看来，NVH性能是一个看不见却又实实在在影响到用户实际驾乘感受的存在，所以NVH性能研发具有极为重要的意义。

"如果说车辆的外观、内饰是车辆的'面子'，那么NVH性能就是车辆的'里子'。"对于自主品牌，李登山有着自己的认识，"中国品牌要想真正赢得消费者，'里子'很重要"。

"当时，公司对红旗车型的产品质量要求提高到前所未有的高度，大家也都感受到前所未有的压力。"尽管那时经手的项目还不多，李登山却有着"初生牛犊不怕虎"的气势。"以红旗H9这款车型为例，在立项之初，我们就直接瞄准同级别豪华品牌的最高水平，就是要和它们掰掰手腕。"李登山说。

立下"军令状"后，加班成了李登山的工作常态，人手一本的《精益工作手册》也越写越厚。他在手册扉页写下自己的座右

Making the Hongqi (Red Flag) Car More Captivating 让"红旗"更加招展

铭——"唯守心中志，一隔弦外音"，激励自己不达目标誓不罢休。

"要掌握核心技术标准，就要建立完整的体系。"通过正向研发，李登山梳理建立了声学包八大数据库，编写了三项集团级标准及多项专业级标准，完善了专业DMU检查表等。

最终，通过45项声学包措施及SEA仿真优化分布，红旗H9隔声目标达成，为实现世界先进水平的风噪（17宋）和路噪（54分贝）提供了基本保障。

"红旗H9声学领域性能达到甚至超过那些国际知名豪华品牌的水平，是一点点实现的。"回忆起泡在实验室里的600多个日日夜夜，尽管直言"这个过程非常艰辛"，但李登山还是用笃定的语气告诉记者："我觉得两年多的付出都很值得。"

从H9、H7品质提升项目，H5，再到HS7，以及红旗E-HS3，工作几年来，李登山负责了5款红旗车型的声学包开发工作。

在他负责的红旗H7项目中，首次使用

115

声学玻璃和前围三明治隔声结构,使整车NVH水平显著提升,风噪声改善约3分贝,怠速噪声改善约4分贝。

如今,为了追回2020年疫情带来的时间损失,李登山马不停蹄地投入到新车的NVH性能研发工作中。"我相信,自己一定会看到红旗在世界舞台迎风招展的那一天。"

握紧汽车强国梦的"接力棒"

在吉林省长春市新红旗大街一号的厂区里转上一圈,人们会发现,与李登山一样忙碌又幸福的年轻身影还有不少。尽管隔着口罩,但"试验进展如何""这个月KPI超额完成"仍然是他们打招呼时挂在嘴边的话。

让这些"红旗人"感到振奋的是,这两年,新红旗以市场化为导向,在品牌塑造、造型创意、产品研发、技术创新、品质质量、营销服务等方面的变革动作全面铺开,并不断深化。

事实上，对于正在尝试高端化突围的自主品牌来说，随着正向研发体系的建立，自主品牌技术"空心化"的印象已经渐渐成为"过去时"。在业内人士看来，在世界汽车产业向"电动化、智能化、网联化、共享化"转型的大背景下，找到属于中国汽车产业的核心竞争力是自主品牌突围的关键。

在研发领域，中国一汽长春总部设立了一批研发机构。在这些机构中，作为未来汽车产业的建设者、体验者和受益人，80后、90后正将个人梦想融入时代发展的洪流，握紧"汽车强国梦"的接力棒。

在智能网联开发院有这样一支"尖锋战队"：他们的平均年龄不到30岁，却要在"无处对标、无援可依"的困难下完成智能网联前沿技术的自主研发。

600多个日日夜夜，这群青年工程师从零出发，写下了30多万行代码。他们完成了从需求设计、软件架构到模型搭建、接口定义的全套文件，提前三个月完成任务。

在新能源开发院电机电驱动研究所，这样的故事同样不胜枚举。被同事称为"自主电驱探路勇士"的王斯博深有感触。

作为电机电驱动研究所试验开发主任，王斯博需要攻克的是长期被国外垄断的技术难关。为了实现电动车加速性能的突破，他负责研发的245kW电驱产品需要采用功率模块并联技术路线，但这项技术此前在国内并无先例，开发起来困难重重。

尽管要"从零做起"，王斯博并没有放弃。"此前这项技术被国外垄断，但我们已经攻克了系统集成的原理。"他为团队成员鼓劲儿，说，"面对难点，一个一个攻克，我就不信我们干不成。"

经过数不清次数的论证、试验、推翻、再论证，王斯博率领大家将技术研发和产品工程设计并行。大半年过去了，245kW电驱产品终于成功下线，并搭载到红旗E115整车上。这宣告了一汽已成功掌握豪华电动车必备的高功率电驱系统设计能力。

2020年，突如其来的新冠疫情给企业正常生产带来很多挑战。李登山、王斯博这样的青年工程师冲锋在前，坚守在研发阵地上，为企业顺利复工复产乃至产业不断升级

Making the Hongqi (Red Flag) Car More Captivating
让"红旗"更加招展

发挥着生力军作用。

"争分夺秒,把落下的进度赶回来!最大限度减少疫情造成的损失。"李登山的这句话道出了不少青年的战"疫"心声。

"红旗的振兴不仅是老一辈汽车人的梦想,也是我们这一代青年的梦想。在创新的道路上,青年工程师必须扛起这份责任。"王斯博如是说。

Making the Hongqi (Red Flag) Car More Captivating

It was just after 8 p.m., and two colleagues had just walked into Li Dengshan's small 15-square-meter dormitory. They each stared at their mobile phones, and only the sounds from the phone speakers could be heard.

Li and his colleagues had made this appointment tonight to watch the livestream of the Beijing public debut of the Hongqi H9 car. It was January 8, 2020.

"Look, look, it's almost at our NVH!" Li shouted, and the two colleagues turned their heads instantly.

"Where is it? Why can't we see the livestream?" Because different livestream platforms had different speeds, the three gathered around Li's phone and soon became quiet again. He held it up high, his hand sweating, and did not dare to put it down for fear of missing the moment.

"Hongqi H9 has attained the international advanced level in terms of wind noise (17 sones) and road noise (54 decibels)." When the performance information of the Hongqi H9 NVH was displayed on the big screen, Li and his colleagues laughed out loud. "Seeing the debut of the Hongqi H9 was like watching my child get admitted into

Tsinghua University," recalled Li, "and it was very satisfying."

Although it was nearly 1,000 kilometers away, Li felt like he was there sitting at the press conference. He'd been waiting for two years and two months for this day.

Focusing on the Highest Level in Research and Development

NVH is the abbreviation used to describe vehicle noise, vibration and harshness. These are highly difficult characteristics to manage in automobile quality control. Data shows that about one-third of car failures are related to NVH.

"An abnormal noise may involve the adjustment of multiple assembly units," Li said. NVH is regarded as an important indicator to measure the quality of automobile manufacturing, and is also one of the major concerns of global automobile brands and parts companies.

Upon graduation from Dalian University of Technology in 2016, Li started work at the China FAW Group Corporation (hereinafter referred to as China FAW) as an analyst for body acoustics and air seals. Not long afterwards, the Hongqi brand ushered in unprecedented reforms and set new goals.

"I've been working at Hongqi during a very historic time." In Li's view, NVH performance is an invisible factor which has a direct effect on the user's driving experience, which makes NVH performance research and development of paramount significance.

"If the appearance and interior decoration of an automobile are its outer part, then NVH performance is its inner part." Li has his own ideas about the domestic brand. "If a Chinese brand wants to truly become the favorite of consumers, the inner part is very important."

"At that time, the company raised unprecedented product quality requirements for Hongqi models, and everyone was under unprecedented pressure." Although Li was not involved with many projects at that time, he showed the spirit of "young people dare to do anything and fear nothing." "Take the Hongqi H9 model as an example. Shortly after launching this project, we targeted the highest level of luxury brands of the same model; that is, we wanted to compete with the best."

After Li wrote a pledge to complete the task within the appointed time, he regularly worked overtime, and the "Craftsmanship Manual" issued to everyone became thicker and thicker. He wrote his motto on the front page of the manual: "I will stay true to my original aspiration and fulfill the task despite any difficulties," encouraging himself to be determined to attain his goal.

"To master the core technical standards, we must establish a complete system." Through active research and development, Li sorted out and established eight databases of acoustic packages, compiled three group-level standards and a number of professional standards, and improved the professional DMU checklist.

Finally, through 45 acoustic package measures and SEA simulation to optimize distribution, the sound insulation goal of Hongqi H9 was attained, providing a basic guarantee for achieving the world's advanced levels in wind noise (17 sones) and road noise (54 decibels).

Making the Hongqi (Red Flag) Car More Captivating
让"红旗"更加招展

"The performance of the Hongqi H9 in the field of acoustics has reached or even surpassed the level of those internationally-renowned luxury brands." Recalling more than 600 days and nights spent in the laboratory, Li said this process was very hard. "We made painstaking efforts for more than two years, but it was well worth it."

Over several years, Li has been responsible for the development of the acoustic packages for five Hongqi models: the Hongqi H9 and H7 quality improvement projects, and the H5, HS7 and Hongqi E-HS3.

In the Hongqi H7 project, he used acoustic glass and dash board sandwich sound insulation structures for the first time, which significantly raised the NVH level and reduced wind noise by about 3 sones, and idle speed noise by about 4 decibels.

To compensate for the time loss caused by the COVID-19 epidemic in 2020, Li continued to engage in NVH development performance of the new car. "I believe I will definitely see a more eye-catching Hongqi car on the world stage one day."

Keeping Working to Realize the Dream of a World-Class Car Manufacturer

Walking around the factory at No.1 Xinhongqi Street in Changchun, Jilin Province, people may see many young people busy and happy just like Li Dengshan. Although they wear face masks, there are some common phrases heard every day: "How is the test progressing?" and "The KPI has been overfulfilled this month."

What inspires these "Hongqi people?" It is the fact that over the past two years, the new Hongqi cars have been market-oriented and rolled out with new branding, styling, creativity, product research and development, technological innovation, quality, and marketing services.

In fact, with the establishment of an original R&D system, the poor impression of domestic brand technology has gradually been changed because of those domestic brands that are trying to develop towards the high end. From the perspective of professionals in the automobile industry, and in the context of the transformation of the world's automobile industry to "electric driving, intelligence, networking, and sharing," finding the core competitiveness of China's automobile industry is the key to making a breakthrough for domestic brands.

In the field of R&D, China FAW Changchun headquarters has established a number of R&D institutions. In these institutions, those twenty- and thirty-something young people who will build, experience and benefit from the future auto industry are integrating their personal dreams into the development of the times, and they keep working to realize the dream of becoming a world-class automobile manufacturer.

In the Intelligent Networking Development Institute, there is a cutting-edge team. Their average age is less than 30 years old, but they are tasked with completing independent research and development of the latest intelligent networking technology "without any benchmarks or assistance."

Over more than 600 days and nights, this team of young engineers started from scratch and wrote more than 300,000 lines of code. They finished a complete set of documents covering requirements design, software architecture, model building and interface definition and fulfilled the task three months in advance.

In the Motor and Electric Drive Institute of the New Energy Development Institute, there are also many stories like this. Wang Sibo, who is revered as a pioneer in independent electric automotive technology, has a deeply moving story.

As the director in charge of experiment and development in the Motor and Electric Drive Research Institute, Wang needed to tackle the technologies that had long been monopolized by foreign automobile companies. To make a breakthrough in the acceleration performance of electric vehicles, the 245kW electric drive product for which he was responsible for researching and developing needed to adopt the "parallel power module technology route," but this technology had no precedent in China, and it was difficult to develop.

Although Wang needed to start from scratch, he did not give up. "This technology has been monopolized by foreign companies, but we have tackled the principles of system integration." He encouraged the members of his team by saying, "In the face of difficulties, we must overcome them one by one. I believe that we will succeed."

After countless verifications, experiments, reversals, and re-verifications, Wang led his team in undertaking both technical research and development and product engineering design at the same time. Over six months later, the 245kW electric drive product was finally made and assembled in the Hongqi E115 car. This announced that China FAW had successfully mastered the capabilities to design the high-power electric drive system used in luxury electric vehicles.

In 2020, the sudden outbreak of the COVID-19 epidemic posed many challenges to the normal production of China FAW. Young engineers such as Li Dengshan and Wang Sibo took the lead in continuing to conduct research and development, playing a vital role in the smooth resumption of work and production of China FAW, and the continuous upgrading of the automobile industry.

"Seize every minute and second to compensate for the loss of time! Minimize the losses caused by the COVID-19 epidemic." Li Dengshan's words express the aspirations of many young people also battling against the negative effects of the COVID-19 epidemic.

"The rejuvenation of the Hongqi car is not only the dream of the older generation of auto makers, but also that of the younger generation. Young engineers must also shoulder this responsibility to continue innovation," said Wang Sibo.

好男来当兵

A Good Man Should Join the Army

作者：郑天然 张圣涛 贾方文
翻译：卢 敏

好男来当兵

2020年秋天，24岁的韩博宇又回到了校园。11月的天气有些湿凉，清晨6点的操场空旷无人。简单热身后，韩博宇深吸一口气，冲向了跑道。

长跑是韩博宇最喜欢的一项运动。他喜欢跑步时那种一步一步、脚踏实地的感觉。曾经，他无数次奔跑于北大的未名湖畔。如今，他穿行在中国人民解放军战略支援部队信息工程大学的校园里。

这是韩博宇为自己选择的一条人生跑道。2018年，北大毕业的韩博宇报名参军，成为陆军第83集团军某旅的一名战士。2020年9月，他成功考上军校，一年后他将从这里毕业，成为一名中尉军官。

"我想留在部队"

陆军第83集团军某旅防化一连指导员

常鹏辉与韩博宇的相识也从一场跑步开始。2019年4月,新兵韩博宇初到连队。下连前,常鹏辉就对这位北大毕业生的名字有所耳闻。他惊讶于"北大的学霸也会来当兵",但如今大学生士兵越来越多,"大概是来当两年兵就走吧,北大学子怎么会留在我们这里",这种念头在常鹏辉脑海中一闪而过。

然而几天后,一场新兵体能摸底考核让常鹏辉转变了想法。

那是连队组织的武装越野五公里考核。枪声响起后,韩博宇第一个冲了出去,他跑得很快,像在全力冲刺,立刻冲到了队伍前面。

不少人为他叫好,但没人觉得他能保持到最后,因为长跑拼的是耐力。但两圈后,常鹏辉发现韩博宇的速度并没有下降。因体力消耗很大,韩博宇脸颊泛红,呼吸急促,但他一直坚持了下来,第三圈、第四圈……直至终点。

"也就是说,抵达终点前的每一步,他都在拼尽全力。"那一刻,常鹏辉忽然意识到,"这个兵很踏实,和别人不一样"。

几个月后的一个晚上,常鹏辉忽然接到

上级任务，需要连夜赶写几份材料，誊抄在册。为了加快进度，必须找人帮忙，他想到"高学历"的韩博宇。

深夜11点，常鹏辉找到了已经睡下的韩博宇，这名"秀才兵"二话没说就答应了。深夜3点，常鹏辉在电脑上写完材料，由韩博宇一直抄到早上8点。第二天，常鹏辉拿到记录本，看到字迹工整又清晰，没有一丝潦草的痕迹。

"他认真，脚踏实地，做事永远百分之百尽力，不会有所保留。"常鹏辉认为，韩博宇用行动为自己的"北大"光环做了注解，"只要他想做的事，就一定会争取做到最好"。

班长邹毫对此深有同感。新兵下连第一周，连队组织朗诵比赛，邹毫决定派这位"秀才兵"出战。比赛前一夜，邹毫发现韩博宇竟然练习到深夜三四点，把整篇讲稿背了下来。第二天的比赛中，韩博宇是全连唯一一位脱稿参赛的。他毫无悬念地拿下了冠军。

"有什么任务，只要交给他，就可以完全放心。"邹毫说。

韩博宇则认为一切都是"本分"。"既然

决定做了，就应该认真对待"。他举了个简单的例子，"就像跑步，你走上跑道了，就要一直向着终点跑去。"

2020年9月，韩博宇以优异的成绩考入军校。常鹏辉对此毫不意外，他始终觉得，"如果全旅只有一个人能考上，那肯定就是韩博宇"。

生活可以有很多种选择

其实，投笔从戎之前，韩博宇也曾有些迷茫。

2018年，即将从北京大学毕业的韩博宇和同学们一样，也面临着不少选择：继续读研、出国、回老家或留在北京工作……大多数同学会选择其一，韩博宇也想过回湖南老家工作，但最终，他走了一条"与众不同"的路——他决定去参军。

韩博宇的父母都是乡镇教师，他从小学习认真、刻苦。小学时，因为一道数学题解不出来，他一直做到深夜12点。2014年，韩博宇以湖南省汨罗市理科第一名的成绩考入北京大学城市与环境学院。但来到北大后,韩博宇发现自己其实很普通。在这所人才济济的国内顶尖高校里,一学期过后,他的成绩就不再像过去那样"稳居第一",他在同学中显得有些木讷。

他既没参加过校园十佳歌手大赛,也没做出什么轰动性的学术研究成果。从大一到大四,韩博宇默默学习,早出晚归,奔走于各个教室和图书馆之间,课余活动只加入了一个乒乓球社团。

他唯一不变的是从小的爱好:跑步。大学四年,每当感到迷茫或苦闷的时候,韩博宇就会去未名湖畔跑两圈,舒缓心情。清早,他看见年轻的学子在湖边大声晨读;晚上,他和许多认识或不认识的同学一起夜跑,路过灯火通明的自习室和热闹的礼堂,感到"原来生活可以有很多种样子"。

毕业季,各种用人单位纷纷挤进北大校园,举办应届毕业生招聘会。银行、地产公司、规划院……种种"光鲜的工作",本是韩博宇和同学们"专业对口"的选择。但韩博宇没去参加招聘会。当同学们忙着投递简历时，他选择了报名参军，"就想去战场，去一线冲锋，想做点儿有意义的事"。

"秀才兵"比别人更能吃苦

来到部队，体能训练是韩博宇要迈过的第一道坎。

到防化一连不久，韩博宇参加防护服穿脱训练。初次接触防护服的他很兴奋，谁知却因体力消耗过快，穿脱防护服的速度越来越慢。

副班长刘如虹急了。他用强硬的语气指责了韩博宇，安排他穿着防护服围着操场跑圈加练。习惯了"校园自由生活"的韩博宇不服，也曾在心里暗暗生气，"大不了待两年就走，你爱怎么说就说吧"。

韩博宇性格内敛，那是他少有的几次情绪外露的时候。刘如虹记得，大概两天的时间里，韩博宇总是闷闷不乐，连喊报告的声音都很小。

几天后，刘如虹来找韩博宇谈心了。两个人坐在宿舍里，刘如虹指着训练场上的战友问他:"来部队是要打仗的,不是纸上谈兵。遇到任务了,防护服都穿不好、穿不惯,怎么去执行任务?"

"其实说要走都是气话,道理想明白了,就知道都是因为自己做得不够好。"如今,韩博宇笑着坦然承认,"说白了,还是动手能力弱,不肯下苦功夫。"

掌心的老茧和十指的倒刺见证了他的"反省"。那天谈心后,韩博宇的心结解开了,"待两年就走"的冲动被他抛诸脑后。他开始主动加训,用午休时间练习穿脱防护服,趁阳光正盛时隔着面罩观察毒剂。训练结束后,他脱下防护服,倒出的汗水把地湿了一大片。

"不要以为'秀才兵'就只会读书。他能在学业上取得突出的成绩,就能在别的地方也下大功夫。"常鹏辉说。如今韩博宇的防护服穿脱时间比大纲标准快了1分钟,他可以拍着胸脯保证防化侦毒的正确率,同年兵里,他的军事素质数一数二。

2020年年初,在班长邹毫的推荐下,韩博宇代表连队参加了全旅组织的军事体育特三级评定。这一次,韩博宇的引体向上首次突破了20个,而刚下连时他一个都拉不上去。

那阵子,韩博宇想尽办法加练。他把20公斤重的哑铃片绑在身上,提着装满沙石的弹药箱跑步。每天午饭前,他都会雷打不动地在单杠上练一阵子。练得最狠的时候,同班下士张浩看到他掌心磨出了血泡,韩博宇却一点儿不在意,戴上手套继续练习。

参加体能评定那天,韩博宇醒得很早。他记得那天很冷,天空灰蒙蒙的,站在训练场上,寒风刮得脸生疼,整个手快冻僵了。

他不断哈气,担心气温低影响成绩。但当他看到排在前面的各连尖子做引体向上都在20个以上时,突然觉得"没啥好怕的"。

"别人都能做到,我凭啥做不到?拼了!"韩博宇咬牙跳起,双手死死拉住单杠。他不再感觉到寒风扑面,不再感到手指冻得刺痛,甚至没有数自己做了多少个,只是在心里默念,"再多做一个,多做一个,不能比别人少"。

"对他来说,优秀是一种习惯。在学校

里是，到了部队也是。"邹毫说，"高素质人才不等于书呆子，'秀才兵'不是只会死读书。事实证明，他对优秀有更高的追求，他比别人更能吃苦。"

两个多月后，韩博宇被选为连队的"尖子比武候选人"。一个周末的下午，他参加体能强化训练，全副武装后又多背了两把枪、六瓶水和两个20公斤重的哑铃片，在阳光下跑了整整6公里。

那是韩博宇跑得最吃力的一次，挑战极限的负重让他几近"崩溃"。但冲过终点的那一刻，围观的战友们纷纷鼓掌，大声叫好，让韩博宇感到了从未有过的骄傲与满足。

"那是胜利的感觉。"韩博宇兴奋地说，"到达终点的那一刻，之前的苦和累都不重要了。"

"另一种战士的样子"

其实，韩博宇也有自己游刃有余的领域。在防化一连，韩博宇的专业是防化侦察，这和他大学时学的内容大相径庭，但学习这回事，他"耐得住性子"。

"以前学的是地理、城乡规划，现在学的是化学，知识不一样，方法是一样的。"有时，韩博宇会觉得"又回到了高三或大学备考时"。他从小适应这种环境：高三时，他每天5点起来晨读；大学期末考试前，他泡在图书馆里一待就是一整天。如今，没有可供通宵达旦使用的图书馆，他就四处借书、买书，从前看的各种小说换成了理论教材，放在床头和桌子抽屉里，以便随手翻阅。

几十种毒剂的反应原理和效果，被分门别类地记在几个厚厚的笔记本里。为了区分，他用不同颜色的笔分开标画，"像极了备考的笔记"。

"如果说在部队里我和别人有什么区别，那就是顶着北大的名头，要让学历转化为实力。"韩博宇承认，他的确铆足了劲儿，"想干出点儿成绩"。他把学生时代的习惯带进了军营，提前预习下个阶段的知识点。每次专业训练后，他还要写总结笔记，把"卡了壳"的内容再背一遍。

他偶尔庆幸，"做了这么久的学生，积

攒了不少背书技能"。韩博宇觉得自己记忆力还不错,知识点背得快,理解得也很透彻,因此他每次专业考试都是满分。

但优势是与付出成正比的。下士张浩曾在晚上熄灯后,撞见过在各个角落加班夜读的韩博宇:会议室、楼道走廊,甚至是水房、淋浴间……

"我想留在部队里"

2020年9月份,韩博宇以377分、全旅第一的成绩考入信息工程大学。消息出来后,韩博宇的战友和同学们在朋友圈里转"疯"了,好友们纷纷向他点赞祝贺,但韩博宇本人却很淡定。

"现在的大学生士兵越来越多,北大毕业参军也没什么。我只是走了一条自己想走的路而已。"经过两年部队生活的历练,如今身着军装的韩博宇皮肤黝黑,身姿挺拔,臂膀结实多了。

指导员常鹏辉有时会想起2019年年底考学提干报名前,他曾专门找韩博宇谈过一次心,"虽然想让他留下,但说实话,大学生士兵退伍安置政策也很不错,韩博宇要退伍回北京,能够拿到一笔数额不小的安置费,还可以解决北京户口,考研也有加分。留下来,他就要去竞争全旅为数不多的考学名额。"

但韩博宇早已迈过"走留"这一关。大四那年,韩博宇曾站在北京车水马龙的西四环路边,望着眼前的高楼大厦,望着行色匆匆的人群。他也曾在晚高峰时见到过学校东门的4号线地铁口人潮涌动,马路上汽车拥堵成长龙,写字楼里亮起成片加班的灯光。繁华的城市里,他感觉"找不到自己"。

"退伍回去,拿到一笔钱,有一个北京户口,这很重要吗?"如今韩博宇平静地反问,他始终记得自己的老师——北京大学城市与环境学院党委副书记张新平说过的一句话:"人生的路很长,关键就是那几个节点。最重要的不是走得快慢,而是走一条对的路。"

半年的集中复习期里,每当学习累了,韩博宇还是会习惯性地去操场上跑几圈。和在北大时不同,这一次,韩博宇感到自己的"目的"很明确:"我想考第一,我想拿到考学名额,我想留在部队里!"

"连队在改变他,他也在改变连队"

常鹏辉希望"韩博宇这样的人"留下。

他记得 11 年前自己刚参军时,战士们大多是高中毕业,"有个大学生士兵都当'宝贝',如今名校毕业生愿意留在部队,绝对是质的飞跃。"常鹏辉语气中有隐隐的兴奋,"这让人们看到,过去说'好男不当兵',现在是'好男来当兵',当兵可以成为一种很好的选择。"

韩博宇自己则很少提及学历。战友问起他为什么要当兵时,他常常这样回答:"我没什么特别的,只是普通的一员。大学生士兵多得是。"

但这"普通的一员",确实给连队带来了一些不一样的东西。"他有一种'温和的力量',连队在改变他,他也在改变连队。"常鹏辉说。像一滴水渗入土壤,他记不清从

A Good Man Should Join the Army
好男来当兵

什么时候开始，连队走廊里互相问好的人多了，"大呼小叫"的少了。

上等兵石益博最近在看《毛泽东选集》。以前，他最爱打游戏，觉得这类书都是"爸爸才看的书"。2020年3月下连，他被分到韩博宇的班，第一次拉开韩博宇床下的抽屉柜，石益博惊呆了。

本该堆放杂物的柜子里塞满书，一本本码放得整整齐齐，"什么都有"。韩博宇涉猎广泛，中国的、外国的，军事类、哲学类……他看《道德情操论》，也看《解放军文艺》。在早已读完的小说《北上》旁，放着一本厚厚的《牛津高阶英语词典》。

"跟他在一起，会不自觉地想要优秀，想变得更好。"石益博加入了韩博宇的"阅读大军"，如今，他发现自己竟对哲学也有了兴趣。

训练时，韩博宇则成了大家的标杆。从收到军校录取通知书到入学中间还有一段时间，韩博宇正常跟随连队参加跑步训练。每当发现有人跑不动，这位"跑步尖子"会刻意慢下脚步，陪在战友身边。石益博记得，有一次加练，他中途觉得太累想要放弃，忽然感到后背一热。转过头，看到韩博宇在他身后半步远的位置，边跑边伸出一只手轻轻推着他。

那次，他们两个一起冲过了终点。

今年新兵下连，韩博宇给全旅新兵做了一场报告。不少年轻的战士记住了这个温文尔雅的"韩班长"，"名校出身，居然科科训练也是优秀"。后来在一次问卷调查中，常鹏辉发现，很多人在"我的偶像"一栏填上了韩博宇的名字。

"他的眼睛里有光"

2020年9月底，韩博宇考取军校的消息传开后，北大邀请他回校做讲座。一身戎装的韩博宇再次踏入昔日的校园，感觉"一切大不一样"。

一个周四的下午，韩博宇在学校一个大会议室里为学弟学妹们讲述了自己的从军历程。正值开学季，北大的校园里又挂起征兵横幅，韩博宇身着迷彩作训服走上讲台。

他讲到在部队负重跑步、加练单杠，虽然只有三言两语，却能感受到这背后的艰辛付出。"你可以想象他是经过了怎样的努力，从一个学生变成一名军人。"两年前，韩博宇瘦弱、腼腆，如今干脆利索，面对众人侃侃而谈。

韩博宇本科时的同学张安迎现在留校读研。再次见到韩博宇，张安迎感到"他的眼里有光"。站在讲坛上的韩博宇自信而成熟。谈到从军，他有说不完的话题。张安迎在他身上感觉不到有些同龄人对未来的迷茫，"你看他的眼睛就知道他对自己的人生规划是很坚定的"。

韩博宇已经找到了义无反顾奔跑下去的方向，但他也清楚未来要克服的困难还有很多。在军校的课堂上，同学们来自五湖四海的各个单位，"陆军的，海军的，空军的……他们说的很多专业知识我都不懂"。

韩博宇明显感到"知识储备还不够用"。"将来带兵打仗，都是联合作战，不懂怎么行！"他又拿出了备战高考时的劲头，成了学校图书馆、自习室的常客。尽管学业紧张，韩博宇依旧会去跑步。一有空闲，他就会出现在校园的操场上，跑一个5公里。

操场外的林荫道下，偶尔有整齐的队伍走过，韩博宇转过头便能看到，那是他未来战场上生死与共的战友。

A Good Man Should Join the Army

In the autumn of 2020, 24-year-old Han Boyu returned to the campus. The weather in November was a bit wet and cool, and the playground at 6 a.m. was empty. After a brief warm-up, Han Boyu took a deep breath and rushed to the track.

Long-distance running is Han Boyu's favorite sport. He likes the step-by-step, down-to-earth feeling while running. He used to run around the Weiming Lake of Peking University many times. Today, he walks through the Information Engineering University of the Chinese People's Liberation Army (PLA) Strategic Support Force campus.

This is the life track chosen by Han Boyu for himself. In 2018, Han Boyu, who graduated from Peking University, signed up to join the army and became a soldier in a brigade of the 83rd Group Army of the PLA's Army. In September 2020, he was successfully admitted to the military university. One year later, he graduated from it and became a lieutenant officer.

"I Want to Serve in the Army"

Chang Penghui, the political instructor of the First Chemical Defense Company of a certain brigade of the 83rd Group Army of the PLA's Army, got acquainted with Han Boyu while the latter ran. In

April 2019, the new recruit, Han Boyu, just arrived at the company. Chang Penghui had heard of the name of the graduate from Peking University. What astonished him was that "an elite student of Peking University also came to join the army". But now, more and more university graduates became soldiers. "Probably, he will leave after two years' service. How can the graduate from Peking University serve longer terms in the army?" This thought flashed through Chang Penghui's mind.

However, a few days later, a physical strength test for recruits made Chang Penghui change his mind.

That was an armed cross-country five-kilometer test organized by the company. After the gunshot sounded, Han Boyu rushed out first. He ran very fast as if he sprinted with all his strength and immediately rushed ahead.

Many people applauded him, but no one felt that he could maintain such speed until the finishing line because long-distance running required endurance. But after two laps, Chang Penghui found that Han Boyu did not slow down. Due to a lot of physical exertion, Han Boyu flushed and gasped for breath, but he persisted, the third lap, the fourth lap...until the finishing line.

"In other words, he did all he could to speed every step before reaching the finishing line." At that moment, Chang Penghui suddenly realized, "This soldier is very steady and different from others."

A few months later, Chang Penghui was suddenly given a task from his superiors and needed to write several reports overnight and copy them in the record book. To accomplish the task on time, he had to find someone to help him. He thought of the highly educated soldier Han Boyu.

At 11 p.m., Chang Penghui found Han Boyu, who had already fallen asleep, and the soldier did not hesitate to agree to do this. At 3 a.m., Chang Penghui finished writing the reports on the computer, and Han Boyu made copies until 8 a.m. The next day, Chang Penghui got the record book and saw that the handwriting was neat and clean, without a trace of scribbling.

"He is assiduous and steady and always tries his best to do things without reservation." Chang Penghui believed that Han Boyu's actions would make his alma mater, one of China's top universities, proud. "As long as he wants to do something, he will strive to do it perfectly."

Squad leader Zou Hao felt very much the same. When new recruits served in the first week, the company organized a recitation contest, and Zou Hao decided to send this soldier with an exceptional education background to compete. The night before the contest, Zou Hao found that Han Boyu practiced until three to four o'clock at night and memorized the entire speech draft. During the contest on the second day, Han Boyu was the only contestant who could speak without referring to his script. He won the championship.

"If you have any task, you can rest assured as long as you assign it to him," said Zou Hao.

Han Boyu believed that doing these was his duty. "Since you decide to do something, it should be taken seriously." He gave a simple example.

"It's like running. When you step on the track, you must run to the finishing line."

In September 2020, Han Boyu was admitted to the military university with excellent scores. Chang Penghui was not surprised by this. He believed, "If only one soldier in the brigade is admitted, he must be Han Boyu."

There Are Various Choices in Life

Han Boyu was a little perplexed before he joined the army.

In 2018, Han Boyu, who was about to graduate from Peking University, had various choices like his fellow students, including continuing to pursue postgraduate education, going abroad, and working in his hometown or Beijing. Most of his fellow students would choose one from above, and Han Boyu also thought about returning to his hometown to work. But in the end, he took a different road — he decided to join the army.

Han Boyu's parents are township teachers. He studied hard in his childhood. When he was in primary school, he couldn't solve a math problem; he kept working on it till midnight. In 2014, Han Boyu was admitted to the College of Urban and Environmental Sciences of Peking University with first place in science in Miluo City, Hunan Province. But after studying at Peking University, Han Boyu found that he was actually an ordinary student. In this first-rate domestic university with so many talented students, after one semester, his grades no longer steadily ranked first as he did in the past, and he seemed a bit inarticulate among his classmates.

He neither participated in the campus top ten singer contest nor made any brilliant academic research results. During the four-year study, Han Boyu studied silently, went out early, and returned late from classrooms or libraries. He only joined a table tennis club among all the after-school activities.

His only unchanged hobby since his childhood was running. During the four-year study at university, whenever he felt perplexed or depressed, Han Boyu would go to the Weiming Lake to run for two laps to soothe his mood. Early in the morning, he saw young students reading aloud by the lake. In the evening, he ran with many known or unknown fellow students, passing by the brightly lit reading rooms and bustling auditoriums, and he felt that there were many ways of life.

Before graduation, various employers squeezed into the Peking University campus to hold job fairs for graduates. Banks, real estate companies, and planning institutes provided attractive job opportunities. But Han Boyu did not attend the job fairs. When his fellow students were busy submitting their resumes, he decided to sign up to join the army. He said, "I just want to go to the battlefield to fight and do something meaningful."

A Highly Educated Soldier Can Endure

More Hardships Than Others

When he served in the army, physical training was the first obstacle Han Boyu had to surmount.

Shortly after he became a soldier in the First Chemical Defense Company, Han Boyu participated in the training of putting on and taking off protective clothing. He was very excited when he came into contact with protective clothing for the first time. Still, his speed of putting on and taking off the protective clothing was slower and slower because of excessive physical exertion.

Liu Ruhong, the deputy squad leader, was worried. He criticized Han Boyu and ordered him to wear his protective clothing to run for laps around the playground for practice. Han Boyu, accustomed to the free life on campus, was unwilling to obey the order and got angry. He thought, "At worst, I serve in the army for two years and then leave. You can say as you like."

Han Boyu is introverted. That was one of the few moments he showed his emotions. Liu Ruhong remembered that for about two days, Han Boyu was depressed, and he even reported his arrivals in a low voice.

A few days later, Liu Ruhong came to talk to Han Boyu. They sat in the dormitory. Liu Ruhong pointed to their comrades in arms on the training ground and asked him, "You serve in the army to fight a war instead of talking about stratagems on paper. When you are assigned a military task, if you cannot wear or be not used to wearing your protective clothing, how can you accomplish it?"

"I said I wanted to leave in a fit of temper. After I consider this matter, I know I'm not doing it well." Han Boyu admitted with a smile, "To put it bluntly, I am unwilling to make painstaking efforts so that I am poor at doing things."

The calluses on his palms and the hangnails in his ten fingers witnessed his introspection. After the heart-to-heart talk that day, Han

Boyu got rid of what was weighing on his mind, and he abandoned his impulse to leave after serving in the army for two years. He began to take the initiative in training more, practice putting on and taking off his protective clothing during the noon break, and observe the toxic substances through a face mask in the hot sunshine. After the training, he took off his protective clothing, and his sweat wetted a large piece of the ground.

"Don't think that a highly educated soldier can only read books. If he can obtain outstanding scores in his study, he will make great efforts to do other things," said Chang Penghui. Today, Han Boyu spends one minute faster than the standard set in the training outline putting on and taking off his protective clothing. He can promise to ensure the correct rate of chemical defense and detection of toxic substances. His military quality is one of the best among the new recruits who joined the army in the same year.

At the beginning of 2020, recommended by squad leader Zou Hao, Han Boyu participated in the military sports special level-three assessment organized by the brigade on behalf of his company. This time, Han Boyu did more than 20 pull-ups for the first time, but he couldn't even do one pull-up when he just became a soldier.

At that time, Han Boyu tried his best to do more exercise. He strapped 20 kg dumbbells on his body and ran with the ammunition box full of sand and stones. Before lunch every day, he would practice on the horizontal bar for a while. When he tried his best to practice, Zhang Hao, a fellow corporal in the same squad, saw blood blisters on his palms, but Han Boyu didn't care at all, wearing his gloves to continue to practice.

On the day when he participated in the physical strength assessment, Han Boyu woke up very early. He remembered that it was very cold that day and the sky was gray, and while standing on the training ground, the cold wind hurt his face, and his hands were almost frozen.

He blew on his hands to warm them and was worried that the low temperature would affect his performance. But when he saw that the top soldiers from different companies did more than 20 pull-ups, he suddenly felt that there was nothing to be afraid of.

"Others can do this, why can't I? I'll try my best." Han Boyu gritted his teeth and jumped up, holding onto the horizontal bar with both hands. He felt neither the cold wind blowing on his face nor the tingling of his fingers, and he didn't even count how many pull-ups he did. He only thought, "Do one more, do more than others."

"For him, he is prone to be excellent. This has been true at university and in the army," Zou Hao said. "High-caliber talents are not equal to bookworms. A highly educated soldier is not interested in reading books only. He sets higher requirements for pursuing excellence, and he can endure more hardships than others."

More than two months later, Han Boyu was selected as the company's top contest candidate. One afternoon on the weekend, he participated in intensive physical strength training. After he was fully armed, he carried two more rifles, six bottles of water, and two 20 kg dumbbells and ran six kilometers in the sun.

It was the hardest run for Han Boyu, and the load that challenged the limit made him almost collapse. But the moment he ran to the finishing line, his comrades in arms applauded and cheered him loudly, making Han Boyu so proud and satisfied that he had never felt before.

"That's the feeling of victory," Han Boyu said excitedly. "The moment I reach the finishing line, it is unimportant that I suffered from pain and fatigue while practicing."

"A Unique Soldier"

Han Boyu also excelled in other areas. In the First Chemical Defence Company, Han Boyu was engaged in chemical defense reconnaissance, which was quite different from what he learned at university. But he could study it patiently.

"I used to study geography and urban and rural planning, but now I study chemistry. Although their knowledge is different, the method of learning it is the same." Sometimes, Han Boyu felt that "I was preparing for exams in Grade 3 of senior secondary school or at university." He has adapted to this learning environment since he was a child. In Grade 3 of senior secondary school, he woke up at 5 o'clock every morning to read. Before the final exam at university, he spent a whole day studying in the library. Now there was no library where he could study all day long, so he borrowed and bought books everywhere. He used to read various novels, but now he studied theoretical textbooks at his bedside or in a desk drawer handy to reach.

The reaction principles and effects of dozens of toxic substances were recorded in several thick notebooks. To distinguish them, he used pens of different colors to mark them respectively. These notebooks are like those used to prepare for exams.

"If there is any difference between me and others in the army, I'm a graduate from Peking University, and I should turn my academic qualifications into my competence." Han Boyu admitted that he was determined to score some achievements. He retained his learning habits at school in the barracks and studied the knowledge for the next stage in advance. After finishing military training each time, he also wrote summary notes and memorized once again the knowledge he did not master.

He occasionally rejoiced and said, "I have been a student for a long time and have acquired a lot of recitation skills." Han Boyu felt that he had a good memory, learned knowledge quickly, and understood it thoroughly, so he got full marks in every military exam.

He had his advantages, but he must make great efforts. After lights out, Corporal Zhang Hao caught Han Boyu reading books in every corner: meeting room, corridor, even water room, and shower room.

"I Want to Serve in the Army"

In September 2020, Han Boyu was admitted to the University of Information Engineering with the best score of 377 in the brigade. Hearing the news, Han Boyu's comrades in arms and classmates shared it on WeChat moments. His friends all gave their thumbs-up and congratulations to him, but he was very calm.

"There are more and more soldiers who are university graduates, and it's not extraordinary for a graduate from Peking University to join the army. I just take my own road." After two years of serving in the army,

Han Boyu, now dressed in a military uniform, had a dark complexion and a straight, muscular build.

Political instructor Chang Penghui sometimes remembered that he had a special talk with Han Boyu before the latter applied to take the exam for promotion to an officer at the end of 2019. He said, "Although I want him to serve in the army. To be frank, the policy for the placement of discharged soldiers who are university graduates is also preferential. Suppose Han Boyu wants to leave the army and return to Beijing. In that case, he can get a large sum in placement fees, have Beijing registered permanent residence, and receive extra scores for the postgraduate entrance exam. If he continues to serve in the army, he will compete to become one of the few candidates to take the exam in the brigade."

But it was not a difficult choice for Han Boyu. During his senior year at university, Han Boyu stood by the bustling West Fourth Ring Road in Beijing, looking at the high-rises in front of him and the people who hurriedly passed by. He also saw the crowd at the subway entrance on Line 4 at the university's east gate during the evening rush hour, traffic jams on the road, and lights in office buildings where employees worked overtime. In the bustling city, he felt he could not find his orientation."

"Is it important to leave the army, get a sum of money, and have Beijing registered permanent residence?" Han Boyu asked calmly now. He always remembered what his teacher and deputy secretary of the Party Committee of the College of Urban and Environmental Sciences of Peking University, Zhang Xinping, said, "The road in life is very long, but there are some key junctures. The most important thing is not to go fast or slowly, but to take the right road."

During the six months of intensive review, whenever he got tired of studying, Han Boyu would go to the playground to run for a few laps. Unlike studying at Peking University, this time, Han Boyu felt that his goal was obvious, "I want to win first place in the exam and become a candidate, and I want to serve in the army."

"The Company Is Changing Him, and So Is He"

Chang Penghui hoped that such soldiers as Han Boyu would continue to serve in the army.

He remembered that when he first joined the army 11 years ago, most soldiers were senior secondary school graduates. "If there was a soldier who was a university graduate, he was treasured. Now graduates from prestigious universities are willing to serve in the army, which is a qualitative change," said Chang Penghui excitedly. "This makes people see that it was said that a good man did not join the army, but now a good man serves in the army. Becoming a soldier can be a good choice."

Han Boyu himself seldom mentioned his academic qualifications. When comrades in arms asked why he wanted to be a soldier, he often replied, "I am an ordinary soldier. There are so many soldiers who are university graduates."

But this ordinary soldier did bring some changes to the company. "He is gentle. The company is changing him, and so is he," said Chang Penghui. Like a drop of water seeping into the soil, he couldn't remember when more soldiers started to greet one another in the company's corridor, and fewer soldiers yelled."

Shi Yibo, a private first class, read *Selected Works of Mao Zedong* recently. He had liked playing games most and thought that only his dad read such books. When he became a soldier in the company in March 2020, he was assigned to Han Boyu's squad. When he opened the cabinet drawer under Han Boyu's bed, Shi Yibo was stunned.

The cabinet, which should be stored with sundry articles, was full of various books piled up neatly. Han Boyu read Chinese, foreign, military, and philosophical books. He read *The Theory of Moral Sentiments* and *People's Liberation Army Literature and Art*. Next to the novel *Going North*, which he finished reading a long time ago, was a thick dictionary, *Oxford Advanced English Dictionary*.

"When I live with him, I subconsciously want to be excellent." Shi Yibo joined Han Boyu's reading team. Now he found that he was also interested in philosophy.

During training, Han Boyu became everyone's benchmark. There was still a period of time from receiving the admission notice from the military university. Han Boyu participated in the company's running as usual. Whenever he found a soldier was unable to run further, this top runner would deliberately slow down and accompany his comrade in arms. Shi Yibo remembered that during the extra training one time, he was too tired and wanted to give up halfway, and he suddenly felt a warm touch on his back. Turning his head, he saw Han Boyu running half a step behind him, and stretched out his hand to gently push him forward while running.

Both of them dashed to the finishing line together.

When new recruits served in the company this year, Han Boyu delivered a speech to all new recruits of the brigade. Many young soldiers remembered this gentle and elegant squad leader Han, who graduated from a prestigious university and also obtained excellent training results. Later, in a questionnaire survey, Chang Penghui found that many soldiers filled in the name of Han Boyu in the column of My Idol.

"There Is Light in His Eyes"

At the end of September 2020, after the news of admission to the military university spread, Peking University invited Han Boyu to give a lecture there. Han Boyu, dressed in a military uniform, once again entered the campus and felt very different.

On a Thursday afternoon, Han Boyu told his young schoolmates about his experience of serving in the army in a large meeting room at university. It was the time the school reopened for the new semester. The conscription banner was hung up on the campus of Peking University, and Han Boyu, wearing a camouflage training uniform, walked onto the podium.

He talked about running with a heavy load in the army and practicing horizontal bars. In a few words, everyone could feel the painstaking efforts he made. "You can imagine how hard he trains to transform from a university student to a soldier." Two years ago, Han Boyu had been thin and shy, but now he was simply agile and talks with ease and assurance in front of everyone.

Han Boyu's undergraduate classmate Zhang Anying was studying at university for the postgraduate. Seeing Han Boyu again, Zhang Anying felt that "there is light in his eyes." Standing on the podium, Han Boyu was confident and mature. When talking about joining the army, he had endless topics. Zhang Anying couldn't find the uncertainty about future he often saw in their peers. "Look at his eyes, and you'll know that he is very resolute in his life plan."

Han Boyu had found the goal of forging ahead without the least reservation, but he also knew that there were still many difficulties to overcome in the future. "Students came from various army units from the army, navy, and air force across the country in classes at the military university. I don't know much of their professional knowledge."

Han Boyu obviously felt that his knowledge was not enough. "In the future, leading soldiers in fighting a war will be joint operations, and I must know how to do this." He works with the same concentration and efforts when he was preparing for the college entrance examination and frequents to the library and reading room of the military university. Even though he is busy with his study, Han Boyu still runs. Whenever he has free time, he will appear on the campus playground and run for five kilometers.

Under the tree-lined road outside the playground, occasionally, a neat team of soldiers walk by. Han Boyu turns his head and can see that they are his comrades in arms who will go through thick and thin on the battlefield in the future.

95后水手的海上成长日志

The Deck Log of a Young Sailor

作者：梁　璇
翻译：薛彧威

95后水手的海上成长日志

20多岁的郑毅有一张"看上去40多岁"的脸。在一个时长12秒钟的短视频里,33张自拍特写记录了他皮肤从黑到黢黑的过程。最初,这张国字脸上还有墨镜遮挡留下的色差,渐渐地,眼周也被黑色占领,两颊的皮肤日益显出肉眼可见的粗糙,太久没洗的头发一撮撮支棱着——这是水手的模样,装扮他的正是照片背景里的大海、烈日和看不见的风。

作为克利伯帆船赛"青岛"号上的大使船员,郑毅的环球航海之旅于2019年9月从英国伦敦起航,经过半年漂流,于2020年3月在菲律宾苏比克湾结束第9赛段航行。当时,"青岛"号在总积分榜上领先第二名20分。

按计划,郑毅将在帆船跨国际日期变更线时迎来两次24岁生日,但鉴于新冠肺炎疫情在全球蔓延,后面3个赛段的比赛推迟进行，他的生日也从太平洋上"挪"到了青岛莱西的隔离酒店里。他几乎每天都会思念漂在海上的日子，因为那艘红色帆船不仅能让他续写郭川、宋坤等中国船长的环球航海壮举，更能让他懂得如何重塑自己。

海上的生活不"吹牛"

2006年，跟随父亲到青岛奥帆中心码头游玩的郑毅第一次见到帆船。参加克利伯环球帆船赛的"青岛"号在人群的欢呼声中驶出码头，这一幕从他10岁起就种在心里。第二年，"帆船进校园"活动让郑毅有了梦想成真的可能，他天马行空地"规划"着未来，包括要参加世界级帆船比赛，但在同学眼中，这是他"爱吹牛"的表现。

15岁，郑毅进入专业队，开始了与风浪为伴的日子。他的曾经被视作"吹牛"的愿望也渐次实现，包括代表中国船员将"青岛"号驶向世界。

相对于平静的海面，暴风雨的到来会让郑毅更加"兴奋"——船只像一片叶子一样被浪推来推去，作为舵手的他必须直面挑战。"大雨像一圈屏障一样袭来，感觉像二维游戏中向玩家移动的磁暴阵，伴随着的风力和船速，雨点打在脸上像小石子一样生疼，掌舵根本无法看清前方。"郑毅记得风雨飘摇的每一帧画面，例如，持续迎风的状态下，船头一遇到浪就会颠起两米高，然后垂直"砰"地落下，船舱内睡觉的人会被这一下惊醒，"就像坐在高速行驶的汽车里突然遭遇急刹。"高度倾斜下，厨房里也噼里啪啦乱响，锅碗瓢盆齐飞，让做饭的人应接不暇，有时会被溅一身热水，做的饭菜倒了一地。

海上温度低时，防寒服下得穿软壳夹克、加绒衣、连体裤、贴身防风背心、羊毛内衣等，即便如此，戴着海豹皮手套的手还是会被冻透。郑毅担心手套内会湿，又加了一个刷碗的胶皮手套。舱内也不好受，因舱外温度极低，人呼吸和排出的热量让船舱像水帘洞一样，不断地往下滴水，郑毅把这经历记录在社交平台上，"睡觉的时候水滴在脸上惊醒，这种感觉别提多难受了"。

远洋航行时，在这艘长70尺（约23米）的大帆船上，最基本的吃喝拉撒也会成为挑断情绪神经的利刃。

船上有20人，但仅有10张床，4或6小时的轮班制情况下，两人分享一张床。船只晃动时，很难生火做饭，偶有机会做一次蛋炒饭，因唯一的灶台火特别小，需要把米饭蒸熟后放到烤箱里烤干才能进入炒饭步骤，"得准备4个小时"。通常，外国船员习惯用牛奶冲燕麦粥，但"地道中国胃"的郑毅很难适应，他在限重20公斤的行李里装了40袋方便面和十几瓶老干妈，撑到上岸时便马上用手机搜抵达城市的中餐厅和中国超市。有时，船员会刻意少吃，"因为上厕所也非常痛苦"。在隔离期间，郑毅通过直播分享船上的日子，"迎风时，船倾斜很大，马桶里的水会溢出来，上厕所20分钟，排水得花40分钟"。

在这次赛程里，最"糟心"的是船上的制水机坏了，淡水瞬间稀缺。"坏了，没水吃泡面了。"郑毅记得，当时船行驶在南大洋，离终点还需航行约14天，船上20个人只有400多升水，意味着"每人每天只能喝一升水"。郑毅表示，有队友会拿着量杯每次接500毫升进行分配，大家都自觉遵守。收集的雨水掺上海水用来煮饭或意大利面，锅碗全用海水清洗，咖啡、茶停止服务。

越没水喝越觉得渴，郑毅一边掌舵一边攒着口水舔嘴唇，但越舔越干，平时喝的海水过滤后尝着味道像汽油的水，变得弥足珍贵。缺水的情况让船上不少人都病倒了，但也因事态紧急，抱着求生意念的他们比第二名提前了一天到达终点。

这些用命交换的经历让郑毅一开口就停不下来，可在奶奶和姥姥心里，这都是要"拿链子把你拴起来，不让你出去"的理由。但郑毅的父亲年轻时曾是一名海军，对于儿子的经历和选择，除了支持更藏不住期待。"我爸经常说他在海上遇到的风浪比我遇到的还大，其实他也知道不一定。"郑毅能感觉到父亲的骄傲，"他的微信头像、朋友圈封面都是我"。

最曲折的航线也许最快

"青岛"号的20名船员平均年龄在40岁左右，来自各行各业，"很多年轻人很难拿出一年时间去完成环球"。船上唯一和郑毅同龄的是一位英国女生，"她从6岁就开始玩儿帆船，很多来自英国、澳大利亚、美国、加拿大的队员都像她一样很早就接触帆船运动，他们大多是爱好者，我们中国的队员则基本是职业运动员"。

郑毅在2017年时就参加过克利伯帆船赛的部分赛段。当时的他性格腼腆，外语是短板，也缺乏远航经验，但来自同龄人的比较触动了他，才为他找到一条迅速成长的航线。

参赛前一年，郑毅曾为清华、北大等高校的学生担任帆船夏令营的教练。学生们在谈论远处的山，有人说了一句"望山跑死马"，这让长期在专业队训练的郑毅莫名感触："都是同龄人，他们收获了学业也能接触帆船，但我除了帆船再拿不出像样的东西。"人生的重新定位来得猝不及防。当时，郑毅对队内一名人大的女生有好感，想主动找她说话时，却发现女孩在用英语和外国教练交流，"当时，韩国学生跟我说话我也只能抽搐着嘴角用微笑回应"，那种尴尬时刻提醒郑毅，"我要改变"。

郑毅花大力气学英语，全方位准备克利伯帆船赛。但真正上船后，他才发现自己的单词量"不到一周就全用完了"。表达的不自信让他的敏感被放大，有时他说到一半不知道怎么继续，外国队员就会眼神涣散地点头用"OK"转移话题甚至转身走开，"感觉被无视了，我就决定不说话了"。在从英国利物浦到乌拉圭途中大概三四天里，沉默的郑毅感觉像自己一个人在航行，"非常孤独"。

退赛的想法像波浪翻涌。长时间不能洗澡，加上盐水浸泡，郑毅身上有些地方出现溃烂，当队友招呼他去前甲板时，他怕风浪太大会加重溃烂，以"我不强壮"为由拒绝；航行到第34天时，从同胞手上得到一包大杏仁，已经对船餐厌恶至极的他一边吃杏仁一边掉眼泪，"豆子大的泪珠，一点儿感情不带，就是生理的反应"。很久他才反应过来自己哭了，"我这是在经历啥？太折磨人了"。

他想起《少年派的奇幻漂流》，觉得派与老虎的单独相处太真实了，"派之所以能坚持到陆地，就是因为有老虎的陪伴。"他把日记当成老虎，一股脑地写下怨气、寂寞、艰辛和些许愉悦。这段时间得熬过去，他想起有次看到五星红旗从主帆上打开的场景，便告诉自己，作为极少数的中国面孔，熬的过程里，至少表现得像点儿样，"我代表的不仅是我自己"。

回到陆地上，郑毅经常会想起在海上的日子，就像结疤时难耐的痒，完全盖住了疼的记忆，而不经意间的成长也鼓励他再次起航。这一次，他决定环球，行李中放衣服的空间被无人机等拍摄设备取代，他要给"老虎"升级，"我要记录下所见所闻，不再为了发泄情绪，更为了让更多人了解帆船和大海。"

第二次参赛，郑毅的英语水平提高不少，已经可以主动为其他成员提供帮助，自信也建立起来。最重要的是，有了沟通的可能，曾经他"看不惯、不喜欢"的人也有了光彩。在船上，69岁的伯特兰曾让郑毅有些怨怼，伯特兰每次经过踩到或踹到郑毅，总是"扬长而去"。但慢慢地,郑毅发现伯特兰行动不太方便,他的身体状况并不适合参加这样残酷的比赛。郑毅记得,早在葡萄牙时,伯特兰就问他:"Frankie,你是青岛人吗?我迫不及待想告诉你我为什么想参加这个比赛,这和我妻子有关。"此前,郑毅就听说过有个船员带着妻子的骨灰来航海,他心想千万不要和自己住一起,结果这名船员就是睡在他下铺的伯特兰。

伯特兰的妻子喜欢中国文化,属龙。伯特兰在他妻子去世前就看到过"青岛"号上的龙。因此,在妻子去世后,伯特兰为了完成妻子的梦想,便在参加环球航行时选择了"青岛"号。在小小的帆船上,像伯兰特一样带着满满的故事来漂泊的人数不胜数,他们的故事也帮助郑毅了解到人生的不同切面。"从A点到B点,有无数种路径,可以走直线,风平浪静,但耗时很长;可以走多段折返,经历巨浪,但风浪的加持也会让抵达的时间最快。选择哪条航线掌握在自己手里。"

这次比赛航行的第8天,船慢慢接近了赤道。两年前第一赛段穿越赤道的往事萦绕在郑毅脑海里，当时的痛苦仍然清晰，这次他已经可以从容面对。他把过去在被窝里痛哭、不敢去前甲板的故事"很骄傲地告诉了他们"，"因为只有对比过去才能看到一个人的改变，但我不会再出现同样的问题。"队员们看过照片后告诉郑毅："两年前你是一个男孩，而现在你是男人了。"

The Deck Log of a Young Sailor

Though Zheng Yi is in his 20s, he has the face of a 40-year-old. In a 12-second short video, there are 33 selfies which record the process of his skin turning from dark to even darker. Parts of his face previously white by wearing sunglasses also turned dark. The skin on his cheeks is rough, and tufts of oily hair prick up on his head — the typical image of a sailor. Also seen are the sea, the burning sun, and the uncatchable wind in the backdrop.

As one of the sailors onboard the "Qingdao" ship during the Clipper Round the World Yacht Race, Zheng Yi began his voyage from London in September 2019. Half a year later, the crew finished the ninth leg of the race at Subic Bay in the Philippines. They were 20 points ahead of the second place in the overall standings.

According to their schedule, Zheng would celebrate his 24th birthday twice as the ship approached and crossed the international date line. But due to the COVID-19 pandemic, the following three legs of the race were postponed. Instead of celebrating his birthday on the Pacific, he had to spend it at a hotel in Laixi, Qingdao under quarantine. Sitting in quarantine, he missed the sea. Sailing was his way of carrying on the proud legacy of famous Chinese captains like Guo Chuan and Song Kun. But it was also a way in which he could write his own legacy.

Life on the Sea

In 2006 when Zheng Yi accompanied his father to the Qingdao Olympic Sailing Center, he saw a sailboat for the first time. The boat "Qingdao" was leaving the tier amid the cheers of the crowd to take part in the Clipper Round the World Yacht Race. The scene took root in the heart of the ten-year-old boy. The next year, the "Sailing into Campus Initiative" provided a chance for Zheng to realize his dream. He began "making plans" for the future, including his dream to participate in world-class yacht races. But in the eyes of his classmates, he was just boasting.

At the age of 15, he entered the professional team and kicked off his career as a sailor. His dreams, once regarded as mere boasting, were now becoming a reality, including crewing the "Qingdao" around the world on behalf of China.

When sailing, Zheng would get excited when a storm came. The boat would be pushed about like a leaf in the huge waves, and as helmsman, Zheng had to meet the challenges head on. "Heavy rain would pour down like a wall of water, like a magnetic storm in a two-dimensional game. Because of the wind and boat speed, raindrops hit my face like small stones, and it was impossible for me to see clearly." He could remember many scenes of racing against the headwind and the bow surging up over two meters by the waves and then dropping down vertically with a "bang" so that those sleeping in the cabins would be jolted awake. "It was just like applying the emergency brake in a fast-driving car." Kitchen utensils would be crashing against each other, and the cook, who was caught unprepared, might be splashed with hot water with all his dishes thrown on the floor.

When the temperature is low at sea, the sailors need to wear jackets, sweat shirts, jumpsuits, wind vests and even woolen underwears. And even in sealskin gloves, their hands can easily get frozen. Zheng is constantly worried that the inside of his gloves would become wet, so he'd add a pair of rubber gloves normally used for dish cleaning.

Staying in the cabin was also uncomfortable. If the outside temperature was very low, the heat generated inside through body heat and human breathing could turn the living quarters into a damp cave, with water dripping continuously. Zheng recorded the experience on his social media account. "When you sleep, water might drip on your face and disturb you. The feeling was terrible."

During long voyages onboard the 23-meter-long ship, daily life can be full of headaches.

There were only ten beds for the 20 crew members, so beds were shared as they worked on four- or six-hour shifts. When the ship was shaking, it was very hard to light a fire to cook. "Sometimes I'd get the chance to make egg fried rice, but the one kitchen stove only gave a small fire. The rice needed to be steamed and then dried using a toaster oven, which could take up to four hours." Foreign sailors would often prepare oatmeal porridge by adding milk, which Zheng found hard to get used to as he had a "typical Chinese stomach." In his luggage with a 20 kg weight limit, he jammed 40 bags of instant noodles and over ten jars of chili sauce. After landing at a port, he would immediately use his phone to search for local Chinese restaurants and supermarkets. Also, sometimes the sailors might reduce their food intake "because going to the toilet was also a painful experience". During quarantine, Zheng shared his days at sea through live streaming with his viewers. "When sailing against the wind, the ship might slant a lot, so that the toilet water would spill out. It took 20 minutes to go to the toilet, and 40 minutes to drain the water."

The most annoying incident during the race came when the water machine broke down, which led to an instant halt of fresh water. "Damn! No water to cook my noodles!" Zheng recalled that they were sailing the Southern Ocean — the waters around Antarctica — and it would take them around 14 days to reach their destination. There was only over 400 liters of water left on board for the 20 crew members, which meant that each person could only drink one liter per day. Some crew members would use a measuring cup to take 500ml of water each time and allocate it, a tacit agreement formed among everyone on board. They collected rainwater and mixed it with seawater to cook rice or Italian noodles and used seawater to clean all the kitchenware. They all stopped drinking coffee or tea.

The less water he drank, the thirstier he became. While steering the ship, Zheng tried to moisten his lips with his tongue, but the more he licked, the drier it felt. The once "gasoline taste" of the water filtered from the sea was now considered a precious luxury. The water shortage caused many onboard to get sick. Nonetheless, it was under these dire circumstances that the crew forged ahead to made it first to the finish line, a full day before the 2nd place team.

When talking about these experiences, Zheng cannot keep his mouth closed. In the eyes of his grandmothers, however, these were all good reasons to "fasten their grandson with a chain and never let him leave." Zheng's father, however, a retired naval sailor, showed a lot of support to his son, as well as expectations. "Dad would often say the wind and waves he encountered at sea were stronger than what I experienced. But in fact, he knows that may not necessarily be true." Zheng could sense his father's pride. "He uses my photos as his WeChat portrait and cover."

A Longer Route May Take the Shortest Time

The average age of the "Qingdao" crew was around 40. They came from all walks of life. "Many young people couldn't spend a whole year on the round-the-world journey." The only other person on the ship the same age as Zheng was a British girl. "She had been sailing since she was six, the same as many of the others from the UK, Australia, the US and Canada, who all had been sailing since a very young age. The majority of them are amateur sailors, compared with their Chinese counterparts who are mostly professional."

In 2017, Zheng Yi had participated in some legs of the Clipper Round the World Yacht Race. Back then he was shy owing to a poor command of English and little experience sailing long voyages. But seeing his peers inspired him, and he improved quickly.

One year before the competition, Zheng was coaching the "Sailboat Summer Camp" to train students from Tsinghua, Peking and other universities. One day, the students were talking about the mountains in the distance, and referred to a famous quotation, which plunged Zheng into deep thought. "We were all around the same age. They had not only acquired academic knowledge, but they could also learn the sport. But for me, except for sailing, there was nothing else to be proud of." It had caught him off guard. At that time, Zheng had developed a crush on a girl on the team and tried to speak to her, only to find her chatting in English with a foreign coach, "At that time, if a student from the Republic of Korea said something to me, I could only respond with an embarrassing smile." This prompted him to "make some changes".

Zheng worked hard afterwards to learn English and also to prepare for the Clipper Race. It was not until he embarked on the ship did he realize that his English vocabulary "had been used up in less than a week". The lack of confidence in expressing himself made him become more sensitive. Sometimes when he had difficulties continuing a conversation, the foreign crew members would look at him with distracting eyes, saying "OK" to change the topic or even turn away. "Feeling ignored, I'd decided not to speak." During the three to four days from Liverpool to Uruguay, the silent Chinese sailor felt "very lonely" as if he were sailing alone.

The idea of quitting overwhelmed him. Unable to bathe for a long time and coupled with exposure to salt water caused him to develop ulcers. When other crew members called him to go up to the front deck, he feared the wind and rain would only aggravate his ulcers and refused. On the 34th day, he got a packet of big almonds from a fellow Chinese sailor. He had been disgusted with the ship food, and cried while chewing the almonds. "I was crying big teardrops the size of beans," he recalled. "But they were not tears of emotion, but from a physiological reaction." He continued to ask himself, "Why am I enduring this? It's sheer torture!"

It reminded him of the film *Life of Pi*. He felt the companionship between Pi and the tiger was very realistic. "Because of the tiger's companionship, Pi finally made it to land." He began to write everything down in a journal, including his feelings of resentment, loneliness, hardship and joy. He said he had to go through this period of time. But he recalled seeing the Five-Star Red Flag waving in the wind on top of the mainsail, and at that moment he'd told himself that as one of the few Chinese crew members on board, he should try to put on a good performance. "I realized that I was representing more than just myself."

After some time on land, Zheng would often recall the days at sea, like an unbearably itching scar covering up his painful memories. But he also realized how he'd grown, and he harbored the idea of setting sail again. Next time, however, he would embark on a round-the-world voyage. The space for clothing in his luggage was replaced by drones and other shooting equipment. "I wanted to record everything I saw and heard, and not for venting my grievances, but to let more people know about sailboats and the sea."

By this time, Zheng's English had improved a lot, which paved the way for him to offer help to other crew members, and also built up his confidence. More importantly, it allowed him to better communicate with others. Those he once disliked now seemed more likable to him. 69-year-old Bertrand was one of these people. Whenever he stepped on Zheng's feet, he would "go away as if nothing had happened". But gradually Zheng found out that he actually had some leg problems. In fact, his condition wasn't fit for such an intense sport. Bertrand had once asked him a question when they were still in Portugal, saying,

"Frankie, are you from Qingdao? I'd like to tell you why I'm taking part in this race. It has to do with my wife." Zheng had heard from others that one of the sailors had brought the ashes of his wife on the journey and prayed not to live together with him. Zheng later realized that sailor was none other than Bertrand, who slept in the berth beneath him.

During life, Bertrand's wife had loved Chinese culture, and her zodiac sign was the dragon. Bertrand had once seen the dragon design on the "Qingdao" before his wife died. After she passed away, he chose this ship for the voyage. Just like Bertrand, there were countless people on board who were here for one reason or another, and their stories showed Zheng different life perspectives. "There are many routes from Point A to Point B. You can take a straight line, but if the wind and waves are calm, it could take you a long time. You can also take a roundabout route, but if you have good wind and waves, you'll finish in the shortest period of time. It's up to you to decide which route to take."

On the eighth day of the race, the ship was approaching the equator. Two years ago, Zheng had crossed the equator during the first leg of the voyage. The painful experience was still fresh in his memory, but this time he felt he could handle anything. He told his crewmates his stories of crying in bed and not daring to go to the front deck "because only by comparing with the past can you see a person's change, and I'll never let the same thing happen again." After seeing the photos, Zheng's crewmates all tell him, "Two years ago, you were still a boy, but now you are a man."

为家乡设计"金山银山"的姑娘

A Designer Bringing Wealth to Her Hometown

作者:胡　林
翻译:薛彧威

为家乡设计"金山银山"的姑娘

长发扎成干练的马尾,不化妆,不穿高跟鞋,爱穿"简单耐脏"的深色衣服,这是90后村支书程桔惯常的"打扮"。而6年前,她是一位出入一线城市高档写字楼的平面设计师。

在湖北省咸宁市崇阳县白霓镇大市村,每天晚上7点多,程桔开始入户走访,"白天大家都在地里忙,晚上最适合商量事,开协调会。"30岁的程桔是大市村党支部书记。2020年,第24届"中国青年五四奖章"名单公布,程桔名列其中。

程桔出生在崇阳县城,从小喜欢画画,大学学的是视觉传达专业,2013年毕业后在广州一家企业担任平面设计师。

她的人生在2014年转了个弯。

那年,程桔休假回到大市村爷爷家探亲。上学时每年寒暑假她都会回来待一阵子。村里正在筹备换届选举。她发现,以前生龙活虎的叔叔伯伯聚在一起在唉声叹气：这些年，随着外出务工的村民越来越多，村里很难再选出年轻的接班人。

程桔的党组织关系在村里，一位老党员动员她"考虑考虑"，竞选留下来，给村里发展多争取些政策支持。

竞选村支书是程桔从来没有想过的。她很喜欢设计工作，按照计划，未来她要留在广州发展。

几天后，程桔去找村干部办事，长辈们再次与她沟通。"村里虽然有20多名党员，但65岁以下的只有五六个人，好几个还常年不在家……""我们年纪大了，身体、精力、思路都跟不上，盼着年轻人能回来，给村里带来些变化。"

村里的老人们最是失落：历史上，这座村庄因毗邻大市河而水运繁华，一度商贾云集，商贸繁荣，还出土过国宝级的商代兽面纹青铜鼓。近些年，周边的村子都富起来，三面环山、缺少耕地的大市村逐渐萧条，成了"空心村""贫困村"。

"他们说话的时候，眼睛都瞄着我，全

是期盼，把我的豪情壮志都激发出来了！"初生牛犊不怕虎，程桔想拼一把。这个决定最初遭到母亲的反对，但她拗不过女儿的坚持。程桔计划，"趁年轻，帮家乡干满三年，有起色了，就回广州做设计师"。

2014年底，年仅24岁的程桔当选为大市村党支部书记。

彼时的大市村，基础设施薄弱，水利设施不完备；没有村委会，村民办事很不方便；村集体经济为"零"；很多贫困户没有收入来源。

程桔设计了"基础设施建设＋产业发展＋全域旅游＋乡村治理"的总体思路。为尽快与400多户乡亲彼此熟络，她利用专业知识设计了便民服务卡，标注自己的联系方式，逐家逐户走访、发放。

大市村河道弯曲，河堤陡峭，道路狭窄，暗藏安全隐患。程桔做的第一件事就是加固河堤，拓宽道路。

程桔的工作随时面临着"想象不到的困难"。有一次，程桔组织村民植树。一名村民突然把刚栽好的树苗连根拔起，称这块地是自己种菜用的。一名村干部上前沟通，没说几句两人就推搡起来，程桔赶紧劝架，却被村民一棍子打在手上。程桔的眼泪一下子就流出来了。她转念一想，"立场不同，自然会有矛盾，还是要多沟通"。程桔知道这个村民家境困难，还患有疾病，有时神志不清。程桔对他批评教育，后来还帮他争取了低保。

以前，大市村没有村委会，谁当村支书，村委会就设在谁家。2015年，程桔开始着手建村党群服务中心。

她联系母校老师和学长，以四合院仿古建筑风格进行规划设计；整合村内各项资源，聘请村里的能工巧匠，边施工边修改图纸，并邀请村民理事会、村务监督委员会全程参与、监督。历时近三年，配有文化广场、休闲养生步道的村党员群众服务中心落成了。

同时，历经数次拆迁、协调，在程桔的争取下，大市村修建起一条直通外界的通道。村民出村再也不用借助邻村的道路了。路修好了，村里发展也迎来了更多的可能。

以往，村里的老人与留守妇女靠传统种植业维持生计，收入微薄。程桔调研后，带领大家流转土地，种植中药材。紧接着，猕猴桃种植基地也建起来了，还引进了年产值150万元的小龙虾养殖基地。村里还申请扶贫办帮扶资金100万元，流转土地150亩、建成光伏发电站。2018年，村里建起扶贫车间，贫困户在家门口就可以务工增加收入。

"桔子来了，村子又重新燃起了希望。"当地一位老人评价。原本，大市村建档立卡贫困户有69户238人，几年下来，贫困发生率由2014年的17.04%下降到2018年的0.15%。

2018年，程桔三年任期已满。是走，还是留？

脱贫攻坚到了关键时刻，系列利好政策陆续下达。程桔想起以前，"想做好一件事好难"。现在，资金、政策都不缺，村里发展难得迎来这么好的机遇，"如果在我手里错过了，我以后肯定会后悔当时的选择"。

程桔放弃了三年前定下的返回广州的计

划。这年换届，她继续当选村党支部书记。

在大市村，穿村而过的大市河上，矗立着一座高171米、跨度76米的渡槽。它于1976年建成，是当时全国第一座石砌渡槽。渡槽跨下，河水飞流直下，宛如瀑布。渡槽建造时没有机器，由数百名当地石匠用块块青石砌成。至今，大市村还有一些熟谙石雕技艺的老人。

能否挖掘村里的文化资源，将石雕技艺传承与村庄旅游发展结合起来？程桔开始了新的设计。

2019年，程桔申请扶贫资金支持，请专家规划设计，大市村开始建造石雕工艺厂。目前，厂房已建好。程桔筹划着等验收交付后，先做出一部分石雕文创产品，供周边美丽乡村建设使用；同时招商引资，为后期运营做准备。

这几年，程桔吃住在村里，几乎没有周末。"只要想做事，事情总是越做越多"。

以前是在城里做设计师，现在换到了田间地头，"一样是在追梦"。她觉得自己对家乡的设计"只完成了30％"。她梦想着通过自己的努力,把大市村打造成一个集休闲旅游、现代观光农业为一体的美丽乡村,让村民与城里人一样,过上幸福生活。

　　回乡当村支书的这些年,亲历村子一点一滴的悄然改变,程桔相信,家乡的田野同样也在陪伴、打磨着自己。

A Designer Bringing Wealth to Her Hometown

She normally appears with a long ponytail, no makeup or high-heels, and dressed in simple, dark clothing. Her name is Cheng Ju, and she is the 30-year-old Party Secretary of Dashi Village located near the city of Xianning in Hubei Province. Only six years ago, she was a graphic designer working in an office building in a top-tier city.

Every evening after 7 o'clock, Cheng Ju begins her visits to each household in the village. "Everyone is busy in the fields during the daytime, so evening is the best time to meet," she said. In 2020, her name was on the shortlist of recipients for the 24th "China Youth May Fourth Medal".

Raised in this area, Cheng had loved painting since childhood. She majored in visual communications at college and began working for a company as a graphic designer in 2013 upon graduation.

But in 2014, her life took a turn.

That year, she was on vacation at her grandfather's home in Dashi. At that time, the village was preparing for the upcoming village elections. She was surprised to see the older men of the village gather together and be distraught. Over the past years, more and more young villagers had left home to earn a living, making it more difficult to find a young person to be the next Party Secretary.

As Cheng Ju was a Party member, it wasn't long before a senior Party member approached her to persuade her to run for Party Secretary so that she could stay and work for more policy support for their hometown.

But the young lady had never thought of running for such a post. She loved her design work and was planning to pursue her future career in Guangzhou.

She met with the village officials for some business a few days later and met with the seniors again. They said to her, "Although there are more than 20 Party members in our village, only five or six of them are below age 65, and several of them are away from home all year round....We are getting older and it's getting harder to keep up our health, our energy and thinking. We're hoping that young people like you can come back and bring some fresh changes to the village."

The old villagers were among the most frustrated. Throughout history, their hometown had been a busy water transport hub where merchants converged and business boomed. It was also where the national treasure relic known as the Bronze Drum with Animal Design of the Shang Dynasty had been unearthed. But in recent years, unfortunately, as surrounding villages became wealthier, Dashi Village was in a slump. With mountains on three sides and little arable land, it had become known as a "hollow and needy village".

"As they spoke, their eyes were fixed on me with so much expectation, and this stirred up my aspirations," she recalled. She felt energized, and wanted to give it a try. In the beginning, her mother strongly opposed the decision, but finally gave in to her daughter's persistence. Cheng Ju made a plan for herself: "Work for my hometown for three years, and when conditions get better, I'll return to Guangzhou to take up my job again as a designer."

At the end of 2014, the 24-year-old was elected as the Party Secretary of Dashi Village.

At that time, the village had very poor infrastructure and lacked water conservancy facilities. It also had no villagers' committee, which made it very difficult to get things done. Also, the collective economy of the village was "zero," and many poor families had no income at all.

Cheng Ju went to work. She designed a development roadmap for her village, consisting of "infrastructure construction + industrial development + all-round tourism + village governance." In order to foster a closer relationship with more than 400 households, she used her professional skills to design a kind of service card upon which she added her phone number and address. Then she began visiting each family and giving out the cards.

Around Dashi Village were many dangers such as winding rivers, steep embankments, and narrow roads. The first item Cheng Ju needed to face was fixing these problems — to reinforce the river embankments and widen the roads. But many "unexpected hurdles" were awaiting her. One day, Cheng led some villagers to plant trees. Suddenly a villager appeared and uprooted all the saplings which had just been planted, claiming that the land was part of his vegetable field. A village official came over to talk with him. They exchanged words and began pushing each other. Cheng Ju intervened, trying to stop them, but was hit on the hand by a stick held by the villager. Tears burst from her eyes, but then she realized that different people would have different perspectives, making conflict hard to avoid. She realized that good communication was the key to solving problems. She knew that the man's family was poor, and he had been suffering from illnesses for a long time, and was known to sometimes lose his senses. Cheng calmly pointed out his mistake, and later helped him obtain minimum living subsidies.

There had never been a villagers' committee in Dashi, with meetings concerning the village taking place in the home of whoever was Party Secretary. In 2015, Cheng Ju began building a Village Service Center.

After seeking advice from former teachers and colleagues of her college, she chose to build the new service center in the style of a traditional courtyard dwelling. By pooling resources of the village, she employed skillful craftsmen for the project. Members of the village executive council and supervisory committee of village affairs were also invited to be involved. After nearly three years, the Village Service Center was completed, along with a culture square and health trails.

While the service center was under construction, a direct road linking the village with the outside world was also built, much to the persistence of Cheng Ju. Because of this road, villagers no longer had to rely on roads of neighboring villages to get out. The new road also provided more possibilities for development.

In the past, the elderly and women used to make a living from simple farming and had a meager income. After a lot of research, Cheng convinced them to circulate their land and grow plants and herbs used in traditional Chinese medicine. Before long, they also set up a kiwi plantation and brought in a crayfish breeding base which currently produces an annual output value of 1.5 million yuan. The village also filed for one million yuan of assistance from the Poverty Alleviation Office who also transferred 25 acres of land to the village and built a photovoltaic power station. In 2018, poverty reduction workshops were launched in the village, enabling the needy to work near their homes to increase their income.

"Since Ju has arrived, hope for our village has rekindled," said a local elderly. Originally, Dashi Village had 69 registered needy households with a population of 238. In a few years, the incidence of poverty dropped from 17.04 percent in 2014 to 0.15 percent in 2018.

In 2018, Cheng Ju's three-year term came to an end. Would she leave or stay?

The poverty eradication drive had entered a crucial stage and a series of favorable policies had been released. Cheng Ju recalled in the past when "it was very hard to accomplish anything". Now, with both funds and policies in place, it seemed a golden opportunity for development. "If I let this chance slip through my fingers, I would regret my decision afterwards."

She gave up the plan she'd made three years ago to return to Guangzhou, and opted to stay. She won another term of office as the village Party Secretary that year.

There is an aqueduct running across the Dashi River in the village, which is 171 meters high and spans 76 meters. Completed in 1976, it was the country's first stone aqueduct at the time. The river flowed down under the aqueduct just like a waterfall. It was constructed without any machinery or equipment, built by local stonemasons with beautiful stones. Even now, there are still some old stonemasons living in Dashi Village.

This inspired Cheng Ju with a new thought: could they tap into the cultural resources of the village by combining tourism with the traditional stone-carving techniques of these local craftsmen? She started a new plan.

In 2019, after obtaining more poverty alleviation funding, she invited experts to map out a plan for the project and began constructing a stone carving factory in Dashi village. Construction of the factory has since been finished. Cheng Ju's plan involved creating well-crafted stone products to decorate the village and nearby countryside. At the same time, they would continue to attract investment for future business.

Over these past years, Cheng Ju has been working and living in the village and has rarely enjoyed a weekend off. "There is always work to be done," she said.

Once a designer in the city, Cheng Jun is now "chasing the same dream" in the field. She said she had only completed 30 percent of the design work in her hometown. It has been her wish to build Dashi Village into a beautiful place featuring both leisure tourism and modern sightseeing agriculture so that the people here can enjoy a happy life just as those do in the city.

A Designer Bringing Wealth to Her Hometown

为家乡设计"金山银山"的姑娘

Having been Party Secretary for several years now, Cheng Ju has witnessed many changes in Dashi. But just as she has seen the improvements in her hometown, she's also seen the improvements in herself.

出版策划：王君校　韩　晖
统筹协调：付　眉　韩　颖　彭　博
策划编辑：韩　颖
责任编辑：杨　晗
英文编辑：卢　敏
封面设计：袁长新
排　　版：北京几何创想艺术设计有限公司
印刷监制：汪　洋

图书在版编目（CIP）数据

出彩90后：我的青春不后悔：英汉对照 /"最美中国人"丛书编委会编著. -- 北京：华语教学出版社，2021.11
（最美中国人）
ISBN 978-7-5138-2192-6

Ⅰ. ①出… Ⅱ. ①最… Ⅲ. ①青年—先进事迹—中国—现代 Ⅳ. ① K828.4

中国版本图书馆 CIP 数据核字 (2021) 第 185522 号

出彩90后：我的青春不后悔
"最美中国人"丛书编委会　编著

*

© 华语教学出版社有限责任公司
华语教学出版社有限责任公司出版
（中国北京百万庄大街 24 号　邮政编码 100037）
电话：(86)10-68320585, 68997826
传真：(86)10-68997826, 68326333
网址：www.sinolingua.com.cn
电子信箱：hyjx@sinolingua.com.cn
北京虎彩文化传播有限公司印刷
2022 年（16 开）第 1 版
2023 年第 1 版第 2 次印刷
（汉英）
ISBN 978-7-5138-2192-6
007900